The Splendour of Venice

---

283 COLOUR ILLUSTRATIONS

8 PAGE FOLDOUT WITH THE PALACES ON THE GRAND CANAL
IN *32* WATERCOLOURS

San Giorgio and the Church of the Salute, Sunset.

STORTI EDIZIONI

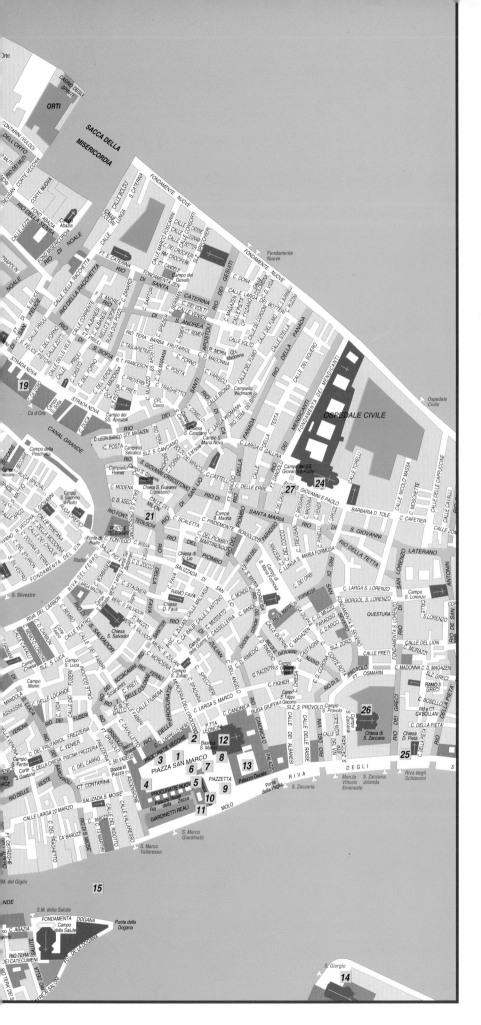

PLAN OF VENICE

(p. 4) *St Mark's Piazzetta.*
Doges' Palace, west facade.

(p. 5) *St Mark's Piazzetta.*
Loggetta and Sansoviniana Library.

This edition contains new illustrations of palaces, canals, and out of the way corners of the city, along with photographs of paintings, art works from museums and private collections, taken after restauration. The accompanying text underlines the most important points of interest. Venice appears illuminated inside and out of the buildings where the Republic's power left its indelible mark; St Mark's Square, the Basilica, the Doges' Palace. In contrast the streets and canals where man and time have had less difficulty transforming and adapting urban space are coloured by a pale light. Some portraits depict people like Marco Polo or Vivaldi, who contributed to creating or spreading Venetian culture. Then, like a trip in time back to the beginning of Venetian history, one finds the Adriatic coast from Torcello to Chioggia including the islands of Burano, Murano, Lido, S.Pietro in Volta. In short this guide intends to help visitors see Venice and take with them a souvenir of this distinctive cityscape.

Venice Curiosities

The Gondola

*I would compare the gondola
to a sweetly rocking cradle,
and the cabin above to a
spacious coffin. It is exactly like that.
We move to and fro along
the Grand Canal, heaving
and surging through life without cares,
between cradle and coffin.*

*"Venetian Epigrams"
J.W. Goethe*

Serenade.

The gondola's form (drawing).

Scenes of "A gondola ride".

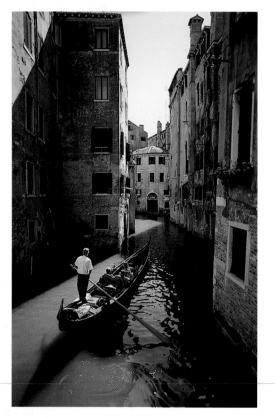

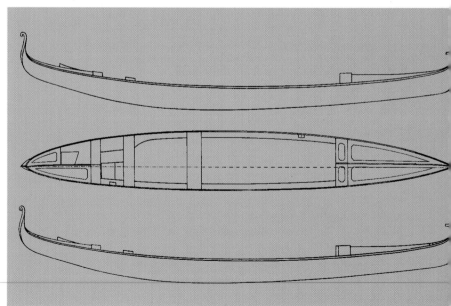

The gondola is long, narrow and asymmetrical: it slides through the water with a zigzag motion the gondolier manipulates to steer the boat. The name "gondola" was first recorded in 1094 and, by the eighteenth century, its present form and dimensions (11.5 meters long and 1.4 meters wide) had already been established. It has a decorative prow, called the *ferro*, and another piece of decorative metal at the stern, both of which are quite elaborate. Gondolas are often adorned with sea horses, with wooden planks painted with floral patterns, or with a *felze* or covered cabin. They can also be upholstered in black felt and decorated with tassels and cords. In the eighteenth century, there were more than 10,000 gondoliers; today there are approximately 500. For many writers and other famous people who have chosen to spend time in Venice, *"a gondola ride"* has always symbolized the city's spirit - and a chance to liberate one's soul from daily routine. There is no doubt that lying back on pillows, listening to the sound of the oars slicing through the water and the calls of the gondoliers, while gliding past the backdrop of noble architecture, contributes to an incomparable feeling of inner peace.

PILE-WORK
ACQUA ALTA

The long-term erosion caused by *acqua alta* (high waters) is one of the phenomena that most threaten the city. It is not easy to describe the awful sensation one has on seeing the tide rise and invade a shop or warehouse (or destroy goods and possessions), yet *acqua alta* has occurred throughout Venetian history. One even finds testimony of it in Paris Bordone's painting *"The Fisherman Presenting St Mark's Ring to the Doge"* now hung in the Accademia Galleries.

The Fisherman Presenting St Mark's Ring to the Doge. Paris Bordone, Accademia Galleries.

Acqua alta in St Mark's Square, Procuratie Vecchie.

Pile-work drawing. Foundations of the Rialto Bridge.

The foundations of the Rialto Bridge. (1) Bulkhead pilings that served as external barriers designed to keep out the canal water. (2) Pilings that supported the zatterone, a kind of pontoon which called for 6000 piles. (3) Zatterone, a pontoon made with planks. (4) Masonry. (5) Average water level. (6) Floor of the canal. The foundations of the Church of the Salute. *"The construction began by driving 1,106,657 oak, alder and larch piles, each about four meters long; it continued over a period of two years and two months. A zatterone made of oak and larch planks securely fastened together was then placed on top of these pilings"* (Sansovino, *Venezia cittá nobilissima* [Venice, the Noblest City], 1663).

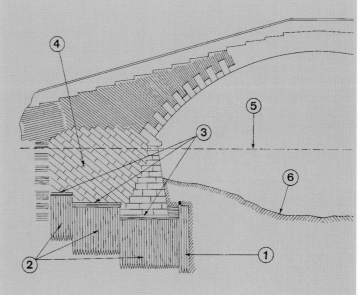

Sebastiano
Ziani
(1172-1178)

Enrico
Dandolo
(1192-1205)

Pietro
Gradenigo
(1289-1311)

Andrea
Contarini
(1368-1382)

With the decline of the Roman Empire, life in the region of Venetia and Histria was threatened by an ever-increasing number of invasions, and its inhabitants started abandoning their homes to seek refuge in the Venetian lagoon. The Lombard invasion of 568 and the capture of both Aquileia and Altino was the last event of this historical process, and perhaps this date marks the birth of Venice. It was from then on that most of the refugees from these and other Veneto cities never returned to their mainland homes. In 584, when the Latin Empire created the Exarch of Ravenna, the lagoon community fell under the rule of Byzantium. The Venetians, who had always supplied salt to the lagoon's hinterland, went on to become successful merchants, sailing and trading farther and farther away from their homeland. This made it necessary to free the upper Adriatic from the threats of the Slavic pirates of the Narenta and to liberate the rest of the sea from the advances of the Saracens. In 991, Doge Pietro Orseolo II landed in Zara and conquered the city's inland territories. Later Doge Domenico Selvo (1071-84) and his successor Vitale Falier (1084-96) defeated the Normans, which further protected trade with the ports of Apulia and helped gain the favour of the Byzantine Empire. As a result Emperor Alexius Comnenus conceded special trading privileges to Venetian merchants. In the period between 1140 and 1160 the role of the doge lost its monarchical characteristics and political power was transferred to the forty-five member Great Council. It was then that the distinctive plan of Venice took shape. The city's political, religious and social functions were concentrated at St Mark's and its commercial centre established at Rialto — the former linked to the latter by the Merceria, the city's most important street. In 1171 Emperor Manuel Comnenus I, with the support of Genoa and Pisa, attempted to expel Venice from the empire, but the Venetians retaliated during the Fourth Crusade by conquering Constantinople, on their mission to liberate the Holy Land. The elderly Doge Enrico Dandolo remained satisfied with acquiring commercial bases, some islands in the Aegean, Modon, Coron and Crete. Meanwhile, the leading families of Venice made ongoing attempts to take over power, with a list of failed conspirators that includes Marin Bocconio (1299), Bajamonte Tiepolo and the Querini brothers (1310), and Marin Faliero (1354). In 1310 the Council of Ten was instituted to check this trend and to inhibit any one patrician family from acquiring too much power. A brief period of peace between Genoa and Venice followed, lasting throughout the late thirteenth century. Battles began again in the fourteenth century, the last of which was fought in the upper Adriatic, threatening the very city of Venice. After defeats at Pola and Chioggia, the Republic, under Captain Vettor Pisani, finally defeated Genoa in a last-ditch effort at Chioggia. Unfortunately, this was not the only threat to the prosperity of Venetian trade, as the Turks had already begun to make their presence felt all across Asia Minor. To compensate for their maritime losses, the Venetians turned towards the mainland where commerce and trade across the Po Valley towards Europe was as important as that in the Mediterranean. The Republic annexed Padua, Treviso, Vicenza, Verona and Brescia. In 1453-54 the Turks, under Mohammed II, gave the final blow to the Eastern Empire, but the territorial ambitions and political importance of Venice were out of proportion with its real forces. The inevitable result was the formation of the League of the Cambrai, which included the Habsburg Emperor Maximilian I, the Kings of France and Spain, the Dukes of Ferrara and Mantua, and was further supported by the Hungarians and the Savoyards. Each had their own reasons for wanting the Republic to fall, and their victory at Agnadello in 1509 represented the total defeat and complete collapse of the Venetian Republic. At the turn of the fifteenth century, the discovery of America opened a new chapter in the history of Europe. The centres of trade moved away from the European seas (the North, the Baltic and the Mediterranean) towards the Atlantic. Tradition usually assigns the beginning of the decline of the Venetian control over trade to this historic moment but, in reality, another hundred years would pass before the trade routes of the Atlantic became truly competitive. Despite ever-increasing difficulty, Venice continued to prosper by importing from the Orient and exporting to western markets. On occasion, the Republic tried to find allies in its struggle against the Turks, but time and again the city was obliged to hold its own. The defeat of Preveza in 1538 and the victory at Lepanto in 1571 were both remarkable and were recorded by the most important painters of the day. The politics of neutrality would be disavowed by exciting, even if useless, pages of history. Only thanks to the intervention of the King of France, Henry IV, did Venice avoid a war with Pope Paul V who had declared an interdict against the Republic, in protest to the arrest of two priests for crimes against the Serenissima. Frà Paolo Sarpi's defense against Bellarmine is a well-known part of the city's history. The point of contention was the city's move to annex Ferrara, the main cause for discord between Venice and the Papacy from the time of Clement VIII until the death of the last Duke of Ferrara, Alfonso II D'Este (1597). The defense of the Venetian-held island of Crete against the Ottomans would be one of the last episodes in which the Republic was able to stave off the course of history. The siege of Candia lasted a quarter of a century, from 1645 to 1669, but in the end even this valuable outlet for the Venetian economy would be lost. Still remaining were Dalmatia and, thanks to the brilliant campaigns of Francesco Morosini, Morea, which was briefly returned to Venetian control by the Treaty of the Karlowitz in 1699 only to be given back to the Turks by the Treaty of Passarowitz in 1712. From then on military and political neutrality became spiritual neutrality. At this point the city was already living in the past. Musical conservatories and casinos sprang up and any occasion was a good excuse for a party. Bullfights and other pleasantries were organized for the dignitaries of foreign delegations; and in some prints of this period one can see the platforms or, rather, the complicated contraptions from which the authorities could view these festive scenes. Towards the close of the century, history was so full of events that the end of the Republic went almost unnoticed: the last Doge, Ludovico Manin, abdicated to Napoleon on May 12, 1797. A form of municipal democracy replaced the republican government, but would last only until October of the same year when, in the Treaty of Campo Formio, Napoleon ceded Venice to Austria in exchange for the left bank of the Rhine and Milan.

Francesco **Foscari** (1423-1457)

Leonardo **Loredan** (1501-1521)

Andrea **Gritti** (1523-1538)

Francesco **Morosini** (1688-1694)

THE FIRST
SETTLEMENTS

*Marciana National Library,
Venice.
The first residential settlements
at Rialto.
16th-century paper codices.*

Venice lagoon.

*Doges' Palace,
Hall of the Scrutinio. King
Pepin's Army, crossing on a
bridge of boats and barrels,
attempting to reach Venice.
A. Vicentino, late-16th century.*

*Jacopo dei Barbari.
Fishing hut.*

The first settlements in the Venetian Lagoon became permanent at the time of the Lombard Invasion (568). It was then that the inhabitants of Aquileia fled to Grado, while those from the south migrated to Torcello and Malamocco, and those from Padua to Chioggia. Remains from this period are scarce. They include the fifth-century oratory at Rialto, San Giacometto, a stone tablet in the Cathedral of Torcello dated 639, the Imperial delegates, the first tribunes of the local administration, King Theodoric's advisor (6th century), Cassiodorus, who described the lagoon's landscape as follows: *"There lie your houses built like sea-birds' nests, half on sea and half on land; and when the aspect of the place changes it looks much like the Cyclades, with those widely strewn houses, not made by nature but rather by the industry of man"* and *"your boats that, like horses, you keep tied up at your house doors".*

THE WAR
AGAINST THE PIRATES

The war against the pirates of Dalmatia and Narenta, from the eastern coasts of the Adriatic Sea, lasted several centuries. During the period of the first settlements, pirates threatened the inhabitants within the very city limits. In order to block their access, heavy iron chains would be strung across the mouth of the Grand Canal and fastened down on both sides of the canal. Later as Venice's power increased, they were checked and even chased out of their safe refuges along the Dalmatian coast. The struggle against the pirates reached a climax under Doge Pietro Orseolo II, who conquered Dalmatia. At that time even the Byzantine Emperor was obliged to recognize Venice's strength, granting her special trading privileges and official recognition, which was then decreed on the Feast of the Sposalizio del Mare (the symbolic wedding of the Doge to the sea). On Ascension Day (*Sensa*, in Venetian dialect), the Doge would sail to San Nicoló on the Lido together with his Signoria and, according to ancient tradition, cast a ring into the sea while reciting the following: *"In segno di eterno dominio, Noi, Doge di Venezia, ti sposiamo, o mare!" (As a sign of eternal domination, I, the Doge, wed thee, my sea!)*

Pushkin Museum, Moscow.
Antonio Canal, known as Canaletto (1697-1768),
The Feast of the Sensa or Sposalizio del Mare.

THE STRUGGLE FOR INVESTITURE

The papal-imperial struggle for investiture fought on the Italian Peninsula during the twelfth century to assert religious and political supremacy did not directly involve Venice. The newly appointed Emperor Frederick Barbarossa came down to the Peninsula to reestablish imperial rights, but the city-states united and formed the Lombard League. With the help of Pope

Alexander III, they were able to defeat the imperial army and consolidate their autonomy. In 1177, Doge Sebastiano Ziani (1172-78) negotiated an end to the papal-imperial hostilities. This historic moment took place in Venice, with the participation of representatives from the city-states, and is recorded in a series of paintings hung in the Hall of the Great Council in the Doges' Palace. Two events that never actually happened are also portrayed: "The Battle of Salvore" and "The Recognition of the Pope in front of the Scuola della Carità". The Pope left these negotiations so satisfied he granted Venice several privileges including the right to celebrate the Feast of the Sensa and to use certain Ducal symbols of authority including a blessed candle, a sword, a faldstool, a canopy, trumpets and eight banners. From then on, this regalia would precede the Doge during ceremonies, as a symbol of the sovereignty of Venice.

CONQUERING CONSTANTINOPLE

At the beginning of the thirteenth century, the eighty-year-old Doge Enrico Dandolo organized, led and carried out the Fourth Crusade (1202-4), with enormously advantageous economic results for Venice. Provisions and galleys for 30,000 men and 16,000 horses were needed for the two-year campaign required to conquer the Dalmatian coast and Constantinople. When the Crusaders had assembled in Venice before setting sail, the Doge expected to be paid the stipulated gold and silver for the transportation and provisions, as had been agreed in a pact made in St Mark's Basilica. The crusaders, however, were unable to pay the price the Doge asked. To further complicate matters, the plague broke out on the Lido, where the men were housed, and some began to abandon the mission. At this point, the Doge decided to accept whatever they were able to pay up front, provided the balance be paid with their alliance. In fact, the Doge and Crusaders reconquered Trieste and Zadar, then Dalmatia, and finally sacked Constantinople. The Crusaders demonstrated an insatiable voracity; the Venetians, who were no less avid, sought more to bring wealth to their city, rather than to themselves as individuals, by taking over strategic trade route ports, as well as works of art, gold and jewels, many of which can still been seen today in Venice.

(Page 16) Doges' Palace, Hall of the Great Council. The Battle of Salvore (1176) Doge Sebastiano Ziani takes Frederick Barbarossa's son Otto prisoner.

(Page 16) Doges' Palace, Hall of the Great Council, courtyard wall. Followers of P.Veronese, Pope Alexander III is welcomed by Doge Sebastiano Ziani in front of the Scuola della Carità.

(Page 17) Doges' Palace, Hall of the Great Council. Francesco Bassano, The Doge receives from the Pope the blessed sword, while the Venetian fleet is about to sail against Barbarossa.

Doges' Palace, Hall of the Great Council (pier-side wall). Giovanni Le Clerc, Doge Enrico Dandolo and the Crusader Captains Swear in St Mark's.

Doges' Palace, Hall of the Great Council (pier-side wall). Jacopo Palma il Giovane, Crusaders under the Leadership of the Doge Assault Constantinople.

THE WAR WITH GENOA

Doges' Palace, Hall of the Great Council.
Two details from Paolo Veronese's painting depicting Doge Andrea Contarini's return from Chioggia.

Doges' Palace, Hall of the Great Council (wall facing the throne).
Paolo Veronese, The Victorious Return of Doge Andrea Contarini after the Defeat of the Genoese at the Battle of Chioggia (1379).

The Venetians and Genoese battled throughout the twelfth, thirteenth and fourteenth centuries for control of Mediterranean trade. The Ottoman Emperors spurred this conflict on by allying at times with Genoa and at others with Venice. After the conquest of Constantinople during the Fourth Crusade (1202-4), Venetian relations with the Ottoman Emperor were complicated by the Turks who preferred the adversaries. Obliged to defend their supremacy, the Venetians attacked and sacked the Genoese at their stronghold in St John of Acre in 1257. The struggle against Genoa lasted for centuries and included the following memorable battles: Genoa's victory at Curzola where Marco Polo was taken prisoner (1268), the Venetian victories at Alghero (1353) and Porto d'Anzio (1378), as well as Genoa's victory at Zara where the Venetian Fleet Commander Vettor Pisani was taken prisoner (1379). After this last battle the Genoese pushed on toward Chioggia, in the Venetian lagoon. The Venetians under Vettor Pisani, however, attacked and annihilated their adversaries, with the assistance of Carlo Zeno's fleet, which was on its way back from the Orient.

ANDREAS CONTARENO DVX,
QVI CLODIANAE CLASSIS
IMPERATOR SERVATA PATRIA,
ATROCISSIMOS HOSTES
FELICISSIMÈ DEBELLAVIT.
M.CCC.LXVIII.VIX.POSTEA AN.XIIII.

ST MARK'S SQUARE
CEREMONIES AND EVENTS

The "castelletti" ceremony. J. Grevembroch.
Correr Museum, Venice.
Castellano and Nicolotto. J. Grevembroch.
Correr Museum, Venice.
Carnival scene, St Mark's Square.
The Doge visits the square in "pozzetto".
Carnival in the Square.

St Mark's Square is the definitive realization and perfection of those spaces traditionally shaped around ancient basilicas. It resulted from the secular evolution to which it was subject in as far as regards both its religious and political constructions. The orchard of the nuns of San Zaccaria and the Batario (Badoer) Canal which occupied and crossed the area were soon transformed and filled in; and the defensive tower, which stood in front of the church adapted for use as a bell-tower. Over the fourteenth, fifteenth and sixteenth centuries the square (the only so-called piazza in Venice) evolved into the ideal gathering place for the city's inhabitants and the perfect representation of Venice for visitors to the city. St Mark's Basilica assumed the responsibility of attracting the population. Its three facades are full of religious elements, statues of saints, artistic sculptures, and ancient traditions to which the inhabitants of Venice came to pray every day, asking to be healed from some disease or for clemency for an imprisoned relative. It is the statue of St Mark, whose body has lain for centuries in the basilica's crypt, which dominates from ahigh the central pinnacle and in whose name the relatives and acquaintances of the inhabitants died at sea and in battle. Beneath the statue and the lion, the symbol of St Mark, one found the four dazzling golden horses representing the strength and power of the Republic. The success of the Fourth Crusade and the conquest of Constantinople were visible to all in the form of spoils from a glorious political and military undertaking. The Venetians were indeed very proud and, in their souls, religious faith and political loyalty grew ever stronger. Religion and politics were what shaped the space and the buildings of the square. The buildings appear to be dominated by empty spaces and there is little vertical development due to environmental conditions, which, at the time of construction, favoured a sense of lightness. Not all visitors to Venice have correctly interpreted these two considerations, but the beauty and charm of the square and that of the city to which they were subjugated spurred one to reflect on the profound and ancient traditions of this city. The wise government of the Serenissima Republic intended the citizen to feel himself an important player, and foreign visitors

to feel a part of contingent events and the affairs of the city. The square has served many a function, from that of church square to that of tournament arena (for competitions like the one Petrarch witnessed from a balcony of the Basilica in 1464), from that of fair grounds for the occasions of celebrations to that of a bull-fighting ring. It has been the backdrop for everything from religious processions to Carnival celebrations.

OFFICIAL VENICE

You can enter St Mark's Square from the south, by way of the Piazzetta, or from the west, passing through the porticoes of the Procuratorie Nuovissime. The Piazzetta is reached from the San Zaccaria water-bus stop or from that of San Marco, after walking along the Giardinetti Reali (the Royal Gardens). If you come from the San Marco stop via Calle Vallaresso, you can enter St Mark's Square from the Procuratorie Nuovissime. For those arriving from Rialto along the narrow shop-filled Mercerie, the wide-open space of the square is spectacular. Both the Piazzetta and St Mark's Square are harmonious spaces defined by open, modest, horizontally-organized buildings whose ample voids are the dominating elements. The buildings in St Mark's Square can be considered in the following groups: first the Clocktower and Procuratie Vecchie, then the Procuratie Nuovissime opposite the Basilica, then the Procuratie Nuove and the Belltower with its Loggetta. On the corner of St Mark's Basilica is the Pietra del Bando. In the Piazzetta, opening to the south between the facades of the Doges' Palace and the Sansoviniana Library, are two tall columns with statues of St Mark and St Theodore. The Porta della Carta is the main entrance to the Doges' Palace; to its left are the statues of the Tetrarchs and the Acritan Pilasters. During the Republic of the Serenissima, St Mark's Square was the city's religious and political centre. It was a space for processions and Carnival celebrations, for ceremonies to elect a new Doge or to receive foreign ambassadors. Today, the square is filled with tourists from all over the world who mingle amongst pigeons, music and the tolling of the bells. The shape of the square resulted from a secular undertaking with its point of reference as St Mark's Basilica. The church is not aligned perfectly with the square because the first buildings were constructed on small separate islands. Around the year 1000, there was a defensive tower in front of the Basilica and the Batario canal across the present-day square in front of the Church of San Geminiano. When, towards 1265, the Basilica reached the dimensions shown in the San Alipio mosaic (in the first doorway of the Basilica on the left), the space in front appeared cramped. At this point, the square was expanded by filling in the Batario Canal and demolishing the Church of San Geminiano. From the end of the fifteenth century until the mid-sixteenth century, the development of the square required the construction of buildings on the long sides and the clearance of the area around the belltower. The shorter side, facing St Mark's, was more problematic for the Doge and the government, who had promised year after year to rebuild the Church of San Geminiano. Jacopo Sansovino finally did rebuild it in the sixteenth century. After several centuries had passed, this shorter end of the square was transformed by Napoleon, who wanted to build himself a large ballroom. He had the Church of San Geminiano demolished and connected the Procuratie Vecchie with the Procuratie Nuove (beginning of the 19th century, designed by the architect Giuseppe Soli). By then the square had taken on the form it has today.

Venice. The Clocktower at night.

Correr Museum. A. .Maccagnini, Portrait of a Noblewoman.

Correr Museum. V. Carpaccio, Young Man with a Red Beret.

Correr Museum. B. Estense, Portrait of a Gentleman.

The Renaissance Clocktower was designed by Mauro Coducci and built between 1496 and 1499. On the top of the tower, bronze statues, known as the Moors (by Ambrogio da le Anchore, 1497) strike the hours. The facade is dominated by a bas-relief of a lion on an enamelled blue background sprinkled with stars. Then there are the statues of the Virgin and Child with the Magi. The Magi are visible only during the Ascension week when they come out and bow before the Virgin. The clock below shows the hours, lunar phases, the signs of the zodiac, and the movements of the sun (by G. Paolo and G.C. Ranieri da Reggio). The Procuratie Vecchie are thought to have been designed by Mauro Coducci and had been built to the first main floor by 1500. They were reconstructed and completed by Bartolomeo Bon, Guglielmo Dei Grigi, and Jacopo Sansovino in 1532. The Procuratie Nuove were built on the site of the former Orseolo Hospice on plans drafted by Vincenzo Scamozzi around 1582; the project was finished by Baldassare Longhena. The interior was divided into apartments for the nine Procurators of St Mark and was later used as Napoleon's Royal Palace. Today they house the Correr Museum and the Risorgimento Museum.

THE PIAZZETTA OF ST MARK'S

"He saw it once more, that landing-place that takes the breath away, that amazing group of incredible structures the Republic set up to meet the awe-struck eye of the approaching seafarer: the airy splendour of the palace and Bridge of Sighs, the columns of lion and saint on the shore, the glory of the projecting flank of the fairy temple, the vista of gateway and clock".

T. Mann, "Death in Venice"

The Acritani Pilasters in front of the basilica's southern facade.
The "pietra del bando" in the southwestern corner of the basilica.
St Mark's Piazzetta, at sunset.

St Mark's Piazzetta. The Loggetta.

Sansoviniana Library.
St Mark's Piazzetta at Night.

The Piazzetta of St Mark's gives onto the lagoon and is flanked by two notable works of architecture, the Doges' Palace to the east and the Sansoviniana Library to the west. At the edge of St Mark's Basin are two monolithic columns brought to Venice from the Levant in the twelfth century together with a third, which fell into the water while being unloaded and was never recovered.

On the bank, known as the Molo, one finds the gondola stations, which are always crowded with gondoliers and tourists negotiating the price of a gondola ride. The Sansoviniana Library was built by Jacopo Sansovino after the Procurators decided to give a dignified home to the manuscript collections donated by Cardinal Bessarion. The facade has a doric ground floor and ionic main floor (piano nobile), and is entirely decorated with friezes and statues. A monumental staircase brings one to the first floor with its anteroom and reading room. The best artists of the day contributed to the decoration of the interior. Titian painted his "Fresco of Wisdom" in the anteroom. On the ceiling of the great hall are works by Jacopo Tintoretto ("The Philosophers"), Veronese, Andrea Meldolla, Battista Zelotti and others. Objects of antique value and beauty, including Byzantine miniatures, ancient manuscripts, Venetian books from the sixteenth century, and the Grimani Breviary are also displayed in this room. At the foot of the belltower is the Loggetta, the entrance to the tower. The function of this Loggetta has varied over the ages. It was built in the sixteenth century by Jacopo Sansovino following the demolition of shops crowded around the base of the tower. It is decorated with bas-reliefs and statues carved by Sansovino and his assistants. On the southwest corner of the Basilica is the Pietra del Bando, from which the decrees of the Republic were read. On the south side of the facade of St Mark's Basilica are the two pillars that were brought here following the conquest of Constantinople in 1204. They are examples of sixth-century Syrian art and have enigmatic inscriptions. Next to the Doges' Palace, on the corner adjacent to the Porta della Carta, one finds the porphyry statues of the "Tetrarchs," which supposedly represent the four emperors at the time of Diocletian and are believed to have been made in fourth-century Egypt.

PROCESSION
OF THE CROSS

"Procession of the Cross in St Mark's Square,"
Gentile Bellini (1496),
Accademia Galleries.

This painting shows St Mark's Square as it appeared at the end of the fifteenth century and allows us to document the changes that have occurred since then. The painting's most important element is the facade of the Basilica of St Mark, which by Bellini's time had been finished and decorated with rare and precious marbles and capitals (the eight above the main doorway were gilt). The arches of the doorways were also covered in gold, and the mosaic cycle in the lunettes depicted the arrival of the body of St Mark in Venice. Today the gilding has mostly disappeared and the mosaics in the four right-hand lunettes were replaced in the seventeenth and eighteenth centuries. Only the left-most doorway, that of Sant'Alipio, retains its original lunette mosaic. The upper-level mosaics in the larger lunettes have also been substituted in recent centuries. In the centre of the facade one finds the four horses of St Mark's. The Procuratie to the left are the low, one-storey Byzantine-style buildings constructed under Doge Ziani. At that time the Clocktower had not yet been built. On the rooftops, Bellini added the characteristic Venetian chimneys, which can still be seen in parts of Venice today. The square was paved with bricks, later to be substituted in the eighteenth century by trachyte slabs. St Mark's Square is shown here with all its pomp and splendour.

THE *PALA D'ORO*

THE *PANTOCRATOR*

The Pala d'Oro is the only masterpiece of the art of goldsmithery left intact in the Basilica, the one object saved from the sacking of the treasury which took place after the fall of the Republic. It is a Venetian Gothic altarpiece assembled by Giampaolo Boninsegna in 1345, re-using the enamels from the previous altarpiece and adding precious stones. The first Pala d'Oro, crafted under Doge Pietro Orseolo I (976-78), was enriched and added to by the Doges Ordelafo Falier (1105) and Pietro Ziani (1209). Even if some of the enamels, gems, and pearls on the Pala d'Oro were presented to Doges by various Byzantine emperors in exchange for assistance provided to them, the pieces of the Pala d'Oro were for the most part fruit of the sacking of Constantinople in 1204 during the Fourth Crusade. The present Pala d'Oro consists of eighty enamels with precious stones mounted on a gold plaque of the dimensions 3.48 x 1.4 meters. The enamels are Byzantine and depict Christian holidays, prophets, apostles, saints and angels as well as the figures of the Empress Irene and the Emperor John Comnenus (1118-45). The figure of latter was partially reworked to portray Doge Ordelafo Falier. The Pala d'Oro should not be thought of as only a priceless ornament for the altar in St. Mark's Basilica, but should also be kept in mind as an inestimably valuable object of pride for all Venetians.

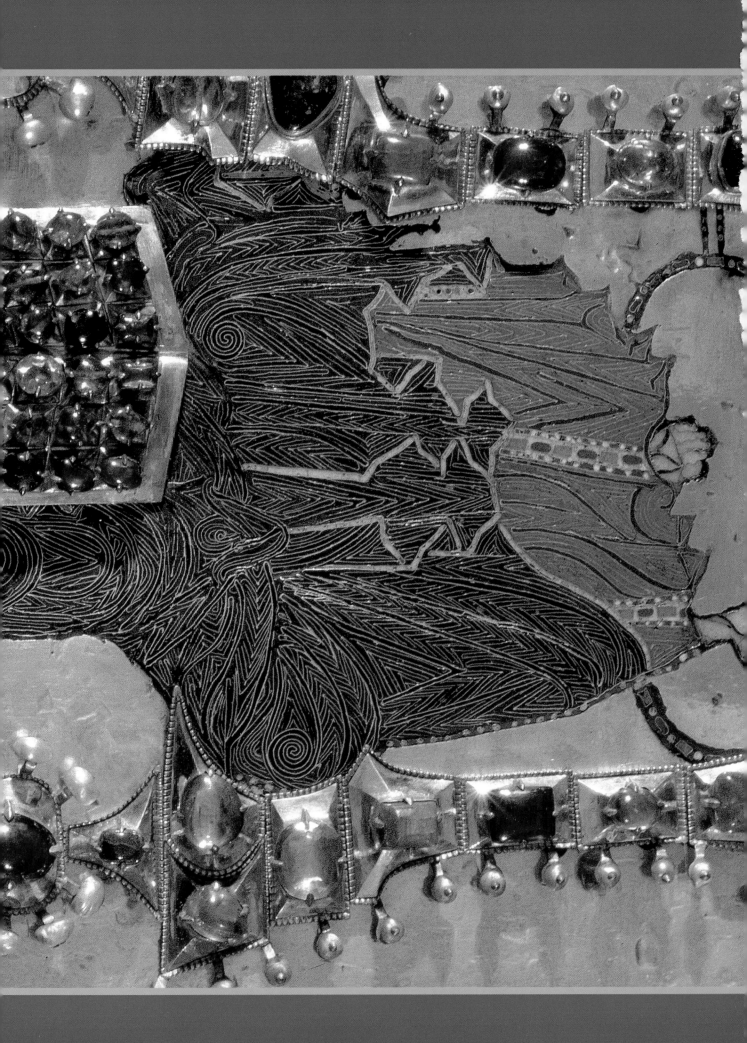

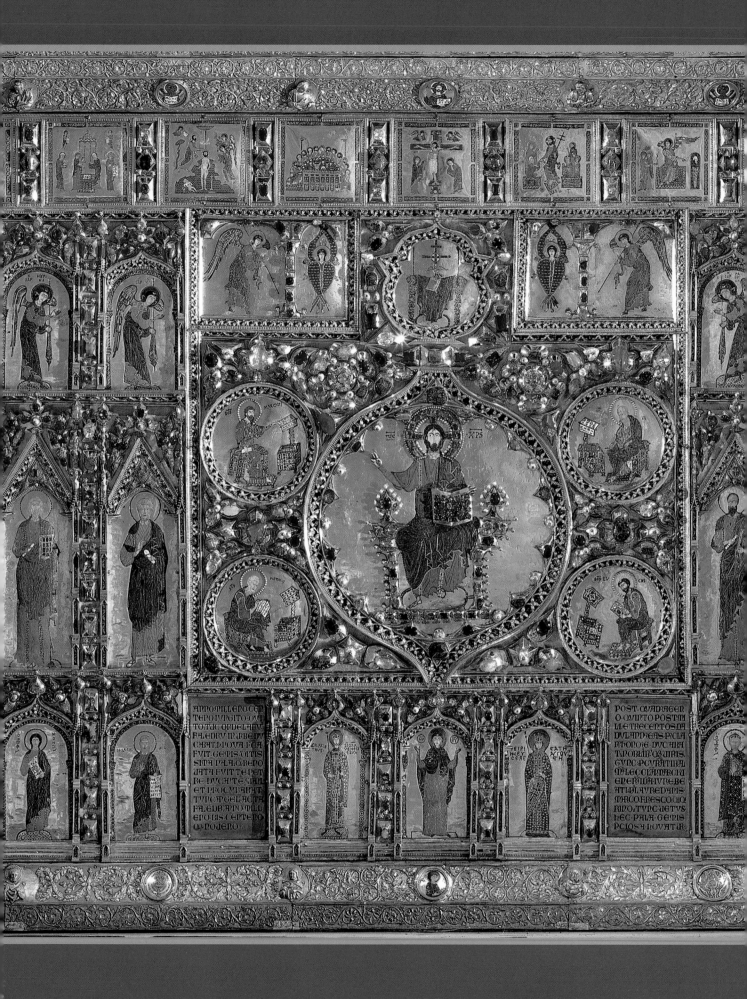

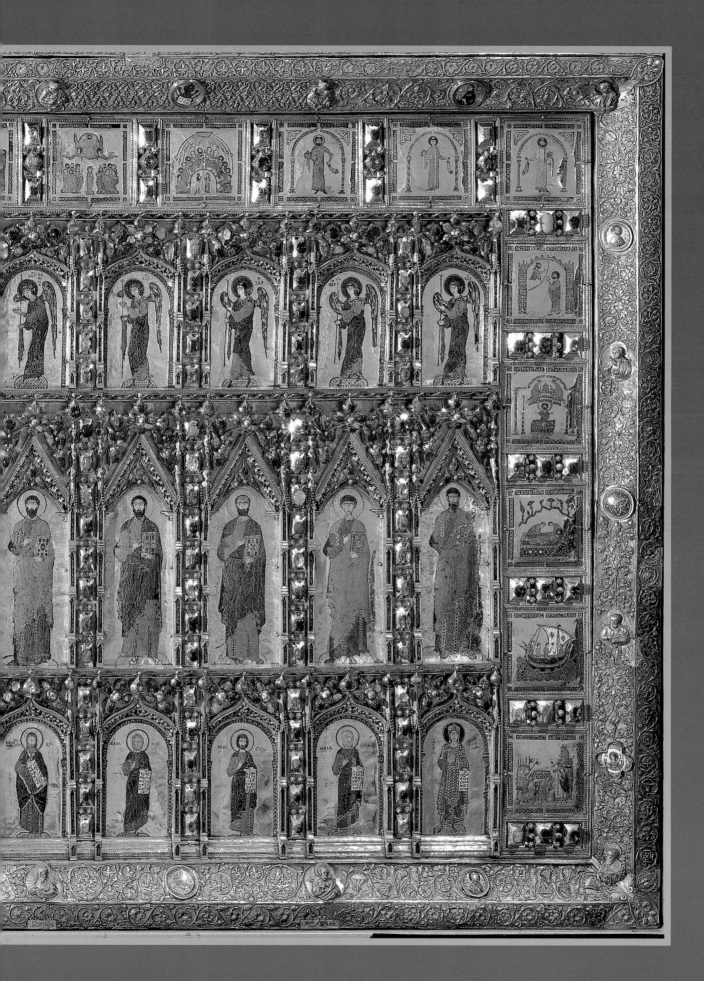

Apse, bowl.
St Mark's, late-11th, early-12th century mosaic.

Mosaics have been used since ancient times to decorate floors, walls and ceilings with various materials including stone, marble, earthenware, ceramics and glass. They are made by attaching tesserae to a drawing done on a base. The different schools of mosaicists can be identified by the size of the tesserae they use, by their method of attaching them to the base, and by their work techniques. The mosaicist can carry out his work completely on site or by using cartoons. In either case a preparatory drawing would always be done in advance. In St Mark's the mosaics are made of glass mixed with gold leaf and coloured marble. The 4000-square meters of mosaic that cover the upper walls and parts of the lateral walls of the basilica were completed over the course of many centuries. The first mosaics dating from the eleventh century can be found in the arch of the central doorway. They depict the Virgin Mary and Apostles. The mosaics in the narthex were part of the original decorative program by thirteenth-century Venetian masters working in a Romanesque style. The cycle begins with the Creation of the World in the first dome on the right in front of the Door of San Clemente. The twenty-four episodes are divided into three bands beginning at the top of the dome and moving downwards. In the first band are the Creation of the Sky, of the Earth, of the Waters, of Light and Darkness, and of the Firmament; in the second band are the Creation of the Sun and Moon, of the Fish and Fowls, of the Animals, of Man and the Endowing of Man with the Holy Spirit, and of God Leading Man to Earthly Paradise; in the third band are Adam and the Animals, the Creation of Eve, Adam and Eve, the Temptation, the Original Sin, the Shame, God Rebukes Adam and Eve, Adam and Eve and the Serpent, the Clothing of Adam and Eve, God Drives Adam and Eve out of the Garden of Eden. The story of Cain and Abel is depicted in the lunette. In the bays next to the central doorway are the scenes of the Great Flood and the Tower of Babel. The latter brings to mind the construction of the defensive tower, later to become the belltower, which stood in front of St Mark's. In the next dome and lunette the Life of Abraham is narrated as follows: Abraham journeys to Egypt; Abraham goes before the King of Sodom; the birth of Abraham's son, a great leader, is foretold; Abraham's wife Sara presents him with Hagar, who will give birth to their son; Ishmail is born; the Birth of a Son to Sara is foretold; Isaac is born. In the three domes in the left wing of the narthex is the Life of Joseph, which includes the following scenes: Joseph's dreams; the sale of Joseph at the market; Reuben, Joseph's oldest brother who knew nothing of what had become of him, finding his cape and mourning the death of his brother; the sale of Joseph to Potiphar, commander of the Egyptian Imperial Guard; Potiphar's wife's tempting of Joseph; Joseph's escaping from Potiphar's wife, his being accused and imprisoned; Joseph's interpreting the dreams of the baker and servant; Joseph's interpreting the dreams of the Pharaoh and predicting seven years' feast and seven years' famine; Joseph as Governor; Jacob sends for grain in Egypt; Joseph welcoming his brother Benjamin and reconciling with his other brothers. In the last dome there is the Life of Moses including scenes of Moses being saved from the waters by the Pharaoh's daughter and the crossing of the Red Sea pursued by Egyptians who later drowned.

The great western arch of the central dome.
The Marys at the sepulchre. 13th-century mosaic.

The first mosaics of the interior are those of the Arch of Paradise, visible from the atrium of the Basilica immediately after the main entrance. Here are the Last Judgment by B. Bozza from cartoons by J. Tintoretto (1577-91); the Damned by A. Gaetano after cartoons by Maffeo Verona (1613-19); the Chosen by G. Marini and A. Gaetano after cartoons by Domenico Tintoretto (1602-09). In the first dome is the Pentecost, a Byzantine mosaic from the late twelfth century, which depicts the Holy Spirit's descent upon the Apostles in the form of tongues of fire. On the lower band of the left aisle are Christ with Four Prophets and the Virgin and Four Prophets, lower band right aisle, (both Veneto School, 13th century). On the upper band of the right aisle we see Jesus Praying in the Garden (13th century). The mosaics in the central dome date from the early-thirteenth century and narrate the Ascension of Christ into Heaven and (in the lower band) depict the Virgin, the Virtues and Beatitudes. In the dome's supporting arches we have Scenes of the Passion with a magnificent Crucifixion from the mid-thirteenth century. On the far wall of the great arch over the left transept are the Life of the Virgin and the Infancy of Jesus, dating from the twelfth to thirteenth centuries. In the great arch of the left transept are the Family Tree of the Virgin by V. Bianchini based on a cartoon by G. Salviati (1542-51) and the Life of Christ, dating from the twelfth and thirteenth centuries. In the right transept is the Dome of St Leonard (or of the Sacrament) with mosaics of St Nicholas, St Clement, St Blaise and St Leonard (early-13th century). On the lower part of the right wall in the right transept is the Finding of St Mark's Body, which includes a stylized representation of the interior of the basilica and the description of the miraculous discovery of the body in 1094. In the great arch above the large Gothic window one finds portrayals of the Four Saints: Anthony and Vincent (by Silvestro after cartoons by Andrea del Castagno) and Bernardino and Paul, the Hermit (by Anthony after cartoons by Paolo Uccello). In the great arch over the Altar of the Sacrament, there are the Miracles of Christ, dating from the twelfth and thirteenth centuries. In the dome over the presbytery appear the Prophets Foretelling the Religion of Christ, from the twelfth century. In the apse cove one finds Christ Offering Blessing, by Pietro Mosaicista, 1506. In the lower part of this area are the patron saints of Venice: St Nicholas, St Peter, St Mark and St Hermagoras (11th–12th centuries). These and the mosaics in the great arch of the central doorway are the oldest and were carried out by artists from the Veneto-Byzantine school as part of the original decorative cycle begun under Doge Domenico Selvo (1071-85). They have been restored many times. In addition to the above-mentioned mosaics, which could be considered the most important, there are also interesting mosaic cycles in the Chapels of the Mascoli and of St Isidore and in the Baptistery, each of which is characterized by a different style and technique. The mosaics in the Chapel of the Mascoli are from the Renaissance (c. 1430). Those in the Chapel of St Isidore are from the mid-fourteenth century and employ narrative mechanisms typical of the Veneto school. The Baptistery mosaics are characterized by their colour, stylization and narrative power. The sacristy is decorated with mosaics from the sixteenth century, which show a great flair for ornamentation imitative of painting.

Right aisle, back wall. Christ Praying in the Garden, 13th-century mosaic.

Mosaic from the Finding of St Mark's body (late-13th century).

ST MARK'S BASILICA

THE RELIGIOUS FULCRUM
OF THE CITY

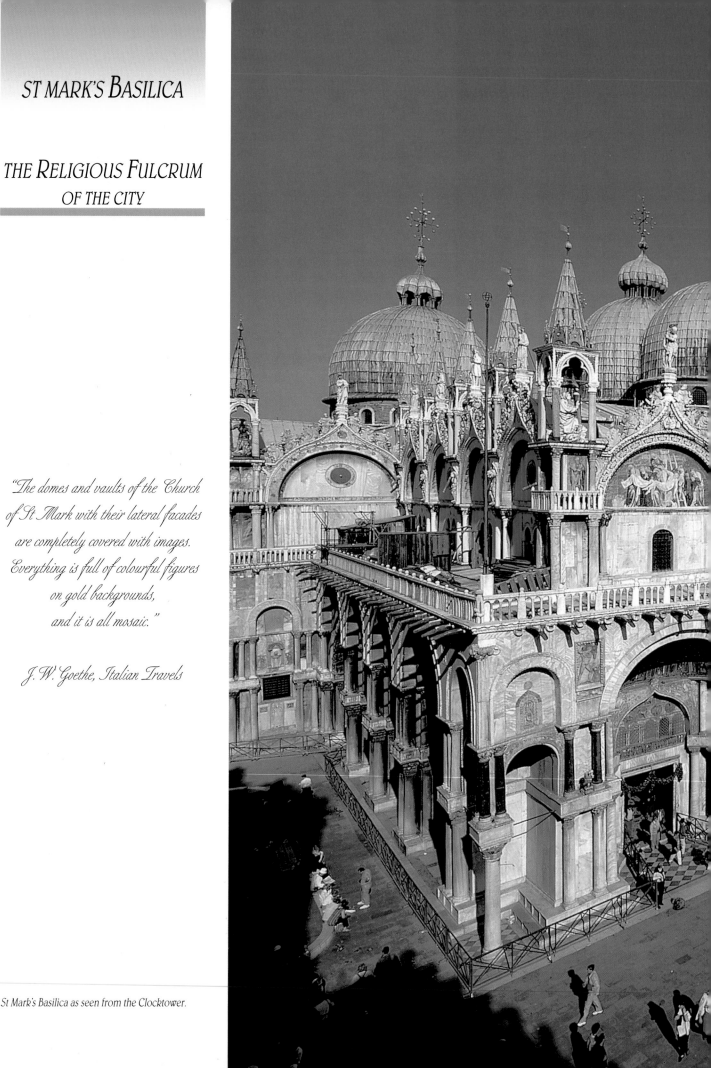

*"The domes and vaults of the Church
of St Mark with their lateral facades
are completely covered with images.
Everything is full of colourful figures
on gold backgrounds,
and it is all mosaic."*

J. W. Goethe, Italian Travels

St Mark's Basilica as seen from the Clocktower.

The church was founded during the ninth century when two merchants, Buono from Malamocco and Rustico from Torcello brought the body of St Mark the Evangelist to Venice from Alexandria in Egypt. St Mark's Basilica was first and foremost the chapel of the Doge. The Doge was responsible for naming the procurators, officers and chaplains of the church. Because of the basilica's dual religious and political function, which would become increasingly evident over the years, it was highly prized and richly adorned with works of art, gold objects, relics and escutcheons of ducal families. Venetians and subjects to Venice alike considered St Mark's as an embodiment of the Republic. It is difficult to identify the few remaining decorations of the original church on this site, that of Partecipazio from 832. The church was rebuilt with the same shape and dimensions as the first in 976 under Doge Pietro Orseolo. The third church was finished in 1071 under Doge Domenico Selvo and consecrated in 1094 under Doge Vitale Falier, and is the church we see today. The west facade has five arched doorways and is divided by a loggia and capped with large Gothic arches with sculptures. At the top of the large central arch is the statue of St Mark and, below, his symbol, the winged lion. As the facade reflects the interior, one could say that it is also the altar of the square, and as such the continuation of the church.

WEST FACADE

The sculptures of the three large arches of the central portal, carved in the thirteenth century by masters of the Antelami school, communicated the reality of life through their symbols, which represent the months of the year, the signs of the Zodiac, the Virtues and Beatitudes, and the Venetian trades. The mosaic of the large Sant'Alipio portal arch is especially interesting because it provides a record of the church facade in the year 1265 (the date it was realized). The other mosaics of the lunettes and arches narrate the events related to the spoils of St Mark. Pietro Vecchia's *Removal of the Body from Alexandria* (first arch on the right) and *Arrival of the Body in Venice* (second arch on the right), both from c. 1660, L. dal Pozzo's *Veneration of the Body by the Signoria* (arch on the left of the central doorway), 1728-29, *the Translation of the Body of St Mark to the Basilica* (second arch on the left). The lunette mosaics in the upper order of the facade (by A.Gaetano after cartoons by Maffeo Verona, 1617-18) depict events from the life of Christ *the Deposition, Descent into Limbo, Resurrection,* and *Ascension.* The bronze doors of the portals date from the thirteenth and fourteenth centuries, the leftmost door bears the inscription, *MCCC Magister Bertuccius Aurifex Venetus.* The Gothic crown with its carved foliage and tracery was begun in the late-fourteenth century under the direction of the Delle Masegne family. Over the years it was further elaborated under the supervision of various sculptors including the Tuscan artists Nicolò Lamberti, his son Pietro, and others from their workshop. At the dawn of the fifteenth century, the art of Florence was undergoing a new sensitivity and taste which would soon give way to Humanism and the Renaissance. This new influence can felt in the Lamberti sculptures.

St Mark's Basilica. Central portal.

St Mark's Basilica. West facade. Gothic crowning (detail).

St Mark's Basilica. Main facade. Sant' Alipio's Portal, mosaic.

The narthex or atrium is a richly decorated part of the church, which is too-often overlooked, perhaps because of the narrowness of its space. We should pause here for a moment to observe its mosaic floor in marble from the eleventh and twelfth centuries. In the centre of the floor there is a lozenge-shaped slab of red marble from Verona that indicates the spot where Emperor Frederick Barbarossa met Pope Alexander III on July 23, 1177. The wall facing the entrance is full of columns with precious capitals. The large number and wide variety of the small and larger columns and capitals in the basilica is due to the fact that there was a secular tradition of ships from Mediterranean ports transporting architectural elements or works of art back to Venice to decorate the basilica and other churches of the city. There are twelve Byzantine marble columns with rare capitals in the form of shells from the eleventh century in the narthex. There are also interesting coupled columns framing the smaller doorways whose capitals are carved with eagles and lion heads which are said to come from the temple of Solomon in Jerusalem. The door of San Clemente in bronze seems to have been the gift of Emperor Alexius Comnenus of Constantinople in the eleventh century.

3

4

5

2

1

6

1 - Dome of the Creation.

2 - Dome of Abraham.

3 - First dome of Joseph.

4 - Second dome of Joseph.

5 - Third dome of Joseph.

6 - Dome of Moses.

St Mark's Basilica,
Central nave.
Dome of the Ascension.
Christ in Glory among Lights
and Stars, The Virgin, the
Twelve Apostles.

Right aisle.
The Virgin Praying
with the Four Prophets,
Isaiah, David, Solomon,
Ezekiel.

ST MARK'S
BASILICA

INTERIOR

The church is organized around the central crossing of the nave and transept in a Greek Cross plan, which means that the arms of the transept are as long as the nave and the presbytery. There are three different floor levels, the lowest being the narthex, then seven steps up to the nave and transept, and finally the highest, the presbytery. The church is oriented along the cardinal points, with the main facade toward the west and the high altar and presbytery to the east, the transept naturally forming a north-south axis. Placing the high altar toward east was part of the tradition of church building and allowed the maximum amount of light to enter and illuminate the mosaics and marbles inside. The interior walls are faced with slabs of coloured veined marbles, and the columns and capitals supporting the upper galleries are also made of marble. Glass mosaics adorn every dome, vault and arch inside the church and cover a total of 4000 square metres.

St Mark's Basilica.
Jacobello and Paolo
delle Masegne,
Rood Screen.

St Mark's Basilica.
Central nave and presbytery.

Dome of the Ascension with the Virtues (foreground); St John and St Luke (in the pendentives) one engrossed, the other showing the Gospel. The figures of two holy rivers (below); the Betrayal of Judas and the Marys gathered around the cross (large right arch); the Baptism of Christ (opposite arch).

PRESBYTERY
HIGH ALTAR
AND
PALA D'ORO

The presbytery with the Rood Screen and the high altar, as seen from the transept.
The windows at the sides of the stairs illuminate the crypt.

It is important to remember that the varying floor levels correspond to the relative sacredness of the different parts of the church, the presbytery being the highest and most holy, raised above the crypt which contains the body of St Mark. The presbytery is separated from the rest of the church by the Rood Screen. This Gothic iconostasis (dated 1394) was carved by Jacobello and Pierpaolo delle Masegne and consists of marble slabs, columns and capitals which support statues of the Virgin, Apostles and St John the Evangelist. In the centre is the bronze and silver cross by Jacopo di Marco Bennato. This isolation of the presbytery is due to its function as the Doge's private chapel. The Doge could enter this chapel directly by way of his own private passageway from the Doges' Palace and hear Mass apart from the rest of the congregation. The floor is a marble mosaic in *opus sectile* and *opus tessellatum* with figures of animals, rhombi, wheels, and some very interesting symbolic geometric motifs. From the pulpit, with its parapets and nine supporting columns in porphyry and jasper, the newly elected Doge would traditionally make his first appearance in public. Opposite this pulpit is a fourteenth-century double pulpit on two levels. The lower level was used for reading from the Epistles and the upper one from the Gospels. This pulpit is covered by a little Oriental dome decorated with fragments of ancient works of art. The Doge would sit at the front of the Presbytery in the Ducal Chair with the Signoria for

celebrations, during which tapestries would be hung on the walls and carpets laid across the floor. In the balconies above the presbytery are galleries for the choir and musicians, which are decorated with bronze reliefs on the parapets by Jacopo Sansovino depicting the Miracles of St Mark. Sansovino also carved the statues of the four evangelists on the balustrade of the high altar (1550-52). Above the altar, there is a ciborium in verd-antique supported by four alabaster columns with reliefs narrating the Lives of the Virgin and Christ. The capitals date from the

*The presbytery with the ciborium supported by sculpted columns
and the Pala d'Oro.*

twelfth century, but the provenance of the columns is uncertain. They are, however, generally believed to be from the sixth century and, because of their stylistic characteristics, to have been carved in the same place by two different artists, one Byzantine and the other from Ravenna. Legend has it that they were brought to Venice from the Church of Santa Maria in Canneto in Dalmatia by Doge Pietro Orseolo II. The high altar is made up of the sarcophagus of St Mark, for centuries conserved in the crypt below. Behind the Pala d'Oro is the Altar of the Sacrament with alabaster and marble columns. Jacopo Sansovino made the bronze reliefs on the Sacristy door, including the Resurrection and the Deposition (1546-69). Sansovino's masterpiece followed a precedent set by Lorenzo Ghiberti in his doors for the Baptistery in Florence. Of particular interest are the portraits of artists of Sansovino's day, who are included in the scenes of the prophets.

The Marciano Museum occupies the area where mosaicists once had their workshops. On display are mosaics by these masters, paintings, lace, tapestries, carpets and other objects. Of note is the Doge's Throne. The balcony on the facade is called the Loggia dei Cavalli because of the four horses which were taken from Constantinople in 1204. The horses on the facade today are copies, the originals being kept here in the Marciano Museum.

The Zen Chapel was built in the south-west corner of the narthex next to the Baptistery in 1504-21 for the tomb of Cardinal G.B. Zen. The extensively restored mosaics date from the thirteenth century. The Baptistery, in the south arm of the narthex, took on its present form in the fourteenth century under Doge Andrea Dandolo (1342-54), whose earthly remains are contained in a funerary monument on the wall facing the entrance. The sixteenth-century baptismal font is the work of Jacopo Sansovino and his students, and the artist himself is buried in front of the altar. The mid-fourteenth century mosaic program narrates the Life of St John the Baptist and the Childhood of Jesus. The Treasury has many ancient and precious objects on display in its three rooms, the Ante-treasury, Sanctuary and Treasury. Each work is well labelled with a description and date. The treasury also tradi-

St Mark's Basilica. The Crypt.

St Mark's Basilica. The Baptistery with the Baptismal Font.

tionally held the Doge's Zoia or Corno (cap) and the crowns of Cyprus and Candia. At the fall of the Republic in 1797, the large majority of precious objects were disassembled and the gold melted down into bars at the mint; other valuables were sold at auction. The most interesting things in the Sacristy of the Basilica are the ceiling mosaics and the inlays on the cupboards. The crypt below the presbytery is a low suggestive space with many columns and precious Byzantine capitals. It has recently been restored and returned to its state of primitive artistic nobility.

THE FOUR HORSES

IN THE
BASILICA MUSEUM

The four horses in the Marciano Museum were taken from the hippodrome in Constantinople during the Fourth Crusade in 1204, but neither their provenance, date, nor even the metal from which they were made is known for sure. Historians have widely varying theories, dating them from the fourth century B.C. to second century A.D., attributing them both Greek and Roman artists, claiming they are made of copper or bronze. What is certain is that for centuries these horses have symbolized the strength and power of the Republic, and that for us today they represent extraordinarily refined and ancient works of art. Napoleon, too, appreciated these horses, enough to take them to Paris with him at the fall of the Venetian Republic. They were fortunately returned to the facade of the Basilica eighteen years later, in 1815.

*School of St Rocco. Titian.
Christ Carrying the Cross.*

*Basilica of Santa Maria of the Frari.
Giovanni Bellini, Triptych. Detail.*

*Doges' Palace, Hall of the College, ceiling.
Paolo Veronese, Venice, Peace and Justice.*

*V*enetian art, architecture, sculpture, painting and crafts began and developed through contacts with Constantinople, which represented the most advanced civilization in the Mediterranean Basin from the fall of the Roman Empire until the conquest of the city by the Turks in the fifteenth century. The Byzantine influence can be seen in the plutei, capitals, vase painting and altar furnishings. Venice was simultaneously in contact with the Western world and influenced by the Romanesque Art of central Italy in Parma, Modena and Verona. In the twelfth and thirteenth centuries, the archivolts in the central portal of St Mark's were sculpted by members of the school of Benedetto Antelami. In the fourteenth and fifteenth centuries local sculptors like De Sanctis, the Della Masegne family and the Bons were active, as were Tuscans like Giovanni and Nino Pisano, Nanni di Bartolo, Giovanni di Martino da Fiesole and Andrea del Verrocchio. From Lombardy and Lugano, there were also Pietro, Antonio and Tullio Lombardo, Mauro Coducci, Antonio Rizzo, and Sebastiano da Lugano. Venetian painting owes its origins to the art of mosaic, which had been practiced in the city for centuries by Byzantine and local masters. As mosaics were declining in popularity, painters Paolo Uccello and Andrea del Castagno came to Venice from Florence and breathed new life into the art of the day. The first Venetian painters whose names are known today are Paolo and Lorenzo Veneziano, Jacobello del Fiore, Michele Giambono, all painting in the Byzantine Gothic Style. There are also the works of Gentile da Fabriano and Antonio Pisano, known as Pisanello. In the fifteenth century Jacopo Bellini and Antonio Vivarini were the heads of the two leading families of painters. The former was the founder of a style of painting which would be perfected by his son Giovanni Bellini. Antonio, Alvise and Bartolomeo Vivarini worked longer in a more traditional Gothic style. The local artists were also influenced by Andrea Mantegna, Carlo Crivelli and Antonello da Messina who introduced the technique of oil painting to the city. Two great painters of the fifteenth and sixteenth centuries were Vittore Carpaccio and Gentile Bellini, who refined the traditional elements of colour and light in paintings that are famous for their transparency and brightness of colour, and for the magnificence of the clothing and the amount of detail. Works by Giorgione di Castelfranco (1478-1510) show the most mature realization of these diverse characteristics. Giorgione's painting was based on the tones of each colour and the relationship of saturation of each, and his work celebrated the beauty of nature in all its manifestations. Every one of his paintings carries a message that emanates from the figures and landscape that was based on the philosophical movement called Aristotelianism, popular in some Venetian circles at that time. The sixteenth century represented a golden age for Venetian art. The works of great painters like Titian, Tintoretto and Veronese made Venetian painting well-known throughout Italy and Europe. Their paintings are visible today in the churches, collections and museums in

Venice and around.the world. Among the important painters of the day were Vincenzo Catena, Giambattista Cima da Conegliano, Francesco da Ponte, Sebastiano del Piombo, Palma Vecchio, Lorenzo Lotto, Pordenone, Paris Bordone, Jacopo Bassano, and Palma Giovane. The seventeenth century marked a period of reduced artistic activity. In the next century, however, with artists such as Piazzetta and Tiepolo or Canaletto and Guardi, Venetian art would enjoy a new prestige. After the fall of the Republic, Venetian artists were influenced by national and international tendencies without ever fully abandoning their roots. To this day Venice remains an important centre for art. The tradition of Venetian building was at first linked to Byzantium. The architectural form of the Venetian palace is organized along generous empty spaces necessary for the movement of goods. On the canal facade, there was an arcade with long, thin columns which allowed for the mooring of boats and unloading of goods; on the ground floor there was a long open hall called androne that had storage rooms along each side. There were also a series of mezzanine rooms above used as offices or warehouses, and the internal courtyard behind the androne was used to store goods. On the piano nobile, there was a large room called a salone or portego, which corresponded to the arch cluster on the facade. Smaller rooms opened off the great hall that were used as kitchens, bedrooms and like. The two-storied fondaco house had a tripartite form and tower blocks at the ends, called torreselle. Venetian church building begins with Santa Maria Assunta in Torcello, a typical Veneto-Byzantine construction that dates from the eleventh century but is very similar in form to the seventh-century church originally constructed on that site (founded in 639). It is on a basilican plan with a wide nave, two smaller side aisles, a chancel, a seventh-century high altar, a raised presbytery and the bishop's throne. The central plan of the Church of Santa Fosca in Torcello with its external arcade is another point of reference, especially since it was built at the same time as St Mark's. Venetian churches belonged to these two types of architectural plans, the basilican plan or the central plan, which was used at St Mark's and Santa Maria Formosa. One of the distinctive characteristics that these three churches share is the foundation layer, which was of little importance except in the case of St Mark's, perhaps because it functioned as the doge's private chapel. The basilican plan became popular again during the Gothic period and was employed in two churches that seem out-of-place in Venice because of their great size, Ss Giovanni e Paolo and Santa Maria Gloriosa dei Frari. During the Renaissance the basilican plan, based on the basilicas of Ancient Rome, was widely used especially in the works of Andrea Palladio (1508-80), whose famous masterpieces include the Church of San Giorgio Maggiore and the Redentore. The Baroque Church of Santa Maria della Salute was the work of Baldassare Longhena (1598-1682) and is centrally planned and raised on a high foundation.

Doges' Palace, Hall of the Antecollege.
Jacopo Tintoretto, Mercury and the Graces.

Palazzo Labia, G.B. Tiepolo,
Cleopatra's Embarkation.

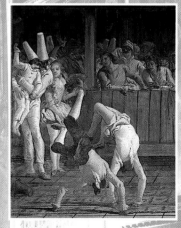

Cà Rezzonico, G. Domenico Tiepolo,
The Clowns.

THE DOGES' PALACE

THE POLITICAL CENTRE

The Doges' Palace is a treasure chest of art works, room after room of carved and gilded wooden ceilings and full masterpiece paintings by famous artists. The spaces are wide of breadth and are both dominated and differentiated by their architectural elements which date from various historical periods. The sumptuousness of the decorative program was intended to reflect and project the wealth and prestige of the Serenissima Republic. The building functioned as the Doge's Residence, Seat of the Government and Hall of Justice. Even if the specific uses of the individual rooms changed over time, offices occupied the first piano nobile and second piano nobile. The second piano nobile also housed the courts of justice, assembly rooms for the magistrates, the Doge's private apartment. The Supreme Court of justice was on the upper floor, on the side of the building facing the canal. On the ground floor and attic storey were the prisons, the latter called *Piombi* because of their notorious lead roofs while the former, the *Pozzi* (Wells), for their location at water

Doges' Palace.
The facade on the Piazzetta.
Every arch on the ground floor
corresponds to two on the first.

level. The kitchens, guards' quarters and service areas were all on the ground floor. The first Byzantine Doges' Palace, begun in the ninth century, was a square building with three towers. In the courtyard, there were separate smaller buildings. This building was destroyed by fire, and in the fourteenth century, a completely new building was begun. Work on the present Doges' Palace started at the Ponte della Paglia and proceeded to the point of the statue of Justice on the facade towards the Piazzetta. The Hall of the Great Council was inaugurated in 1419 and then decorated with a painting cycle that was later destroyed in another fire. After a brief interruption, the building was completed up to the Porta della Carta, which was finished in 1438. In the late fifteenth century, Antonio Rizzo carved the Foscari Arch and Giants' Staircase (1488). After these projects were finished, the wing facing the canal was built, then the Courtyard of the Senators and finally the seventeenth-century Clock Facade by Bartolomeo Monopola, on the north side of the courtyard.

View of the Basilica-Palace architectural complex.

Doges' Palace. Facade on the Piazzetta and the Porta della Carta, as seen from the Loggetta. In the foreground the Loggetta gate by Antonio Gai.

THE DOGES' PALACE

FACADES AND PORTICO

Corner sculpture near the Ponte della Paglia depicting The Drunkenness of Noah.

Detail of a 14th-century capital on the ground floor portraying a wise man.

Hall of the Great Council. Anonymous painting recalling the fire in the Doges' Palace.

Sculpture of Adam and Eve, at the corner of the Riva and the Piazzetta.

Sculpture of the Judgement of Solomon, at the corner near the Porta della Carta.

The Gothic facades of the palace's exterior represent an original sort of architectural style. The portico and upper loggia extend across the entire width of the facades on the Riva degli Schiavoni and the Piazzetta, forming a pattern of solids and very dominant voids and allowing light and air to enter freely. The upper walls are faced with white and pink marble rhombi and are perforated by large arched windows on the second piano nobile and by smaller quatrefoil windows at the attic storey. The cornice is decorated with airy crenelations and pinnacles. The building has an overall lightness to it which betrays an Eastern influence. The thirty-eight columns of the ground floor loggia bear iconographically and symbolically interesting capitals carved with animals, birds, men, women, wise men, emperors, vices and virtues, the trades, and the ages of man. The original capitals,

one different from the next, are on display on the ground floor (west side) of the Doges' Palace. The sculptural groups on the facade's three corners depict subjects laden with symbolism. On the southeast corner, near the Ponte della Paglia, there are the Archangel Raphael and Tobias, the symbol of commerce, and below, the fourteenth-century Drunkenness of Noah, where the sons of Noah try to cover his nakedness, a symbol of tolerance (Matteo Raverti). The groups at the southeast corner show Michael, the Archangel of War, and Adam and Eve with the serpent, symbol of human weakness (late fourteenth century). On the corner nearest the Porta della Carta, there are two fifteenth-century sculptures, Gabriel, Archangel of Peace (by B. Bon) and the Judgment of Solomon, symbol of good government (by the School of Lamberti or Nanni di Bartolo).

St Mark's Basilica, south facade. The Tetrarchs.

Porta della Carta. Head of Justice.
Porta della Carta. Courtly Entrance to the Doges' Palace.

PORTA DELLA CARTA

THE GIANTS' STAIRCASE

The Porta della Carta is famous for its sculptures, statues and busts, and its variety of marbles. During the Republic it was gilded. The sculptures include statues of the Virtues, the bust of Doge Francesco Foscari (copy) kneeling before the winged lion on the architrave, a bust of St Mark in a tondo above, and the statue of Justice at the pinnacle. Bartolomeo Bon carved this Flamboyant Gothic masterpiece, which served as the entrance to the Doges' Palace. The portico, reached through the Porta della Carta, rests against the exterior wall of the St Mark's Basilica, and terminates in the Foscari Arch (A. Bregno, A. Rizzo). In niches on this arch once stood the white marble statues of Adam and Eve by Antonio Rizzo, now on display inside the Doges' Palace. Opposite the Foscari Portico is the Scala dei Giganti, which literally means the Giants' Staircase, which refers to Jacopo Sansovino's enormous sixteenth-century statues of Neptune and Mars (the gods of sea and war) that stand at the top. The staircase is an especially harmonious balance of architecture and sculpture. The bronze inlays on the steps, the openwork and bas-reliefs on the parapets are all exceptional. On the landing below the symbol of St Mark, the newly elected Doge would pledge his allegiance to the Venetian Republic and then be crowned.

COURTYARD
THE RENAISSANCE FACADE

The Giants' Staircase seen from the Foscari loggia.

The courtyard facade in Renaissance style.

The large courtyard has striped marble flooring which marks off the places where the various magistrates stood during official ceremonies. There are two sixteenth-century bronze well heads by Alfonso Alberghetti and Nicolò dei Conti. Having entered the Porta della Carta, we pass through a portico facing the Giants' Staircase, then go up the Scala d'Oro (Golden Staircase) which from the first landing leads right to the Doge's private apartment and meeting halls. The Golden Staircase was used as an entrance on official occasions and, in keeping with its role and name, is richly decorated with frescoes and stucco-work. This staircase was designed by Jacopo Sansovino; the decorative program was carried out by Alessandro Vittoria and G.B. Franco in 1566.

The rooms in the Doge's private apartment are ordered as follows. First, there is the Sala degli Scarlatti, named for the scarlet robes the magistrates donned in this room before going in procession with the Doge. Then comes the Salone dello Scudo (Room of the Crest), named for the family arms of the Doge in office which would hang here. (The family crest of the last Doge now hangs here.) Then, there are the Sala Grimani, Sala Erizzo, Sala degli Stucchi or Priuli (Room of the Stuccoes) and the very large Sala dei Filosofi (Room of the Philosophers), named after the painting *"The Philosophers"* by Jacopo Tintoretto, which once hung here and is now in the Sansoviniana Library. In the staircase from the Room of the Philosophers to the third floor, we find Titian's famous *"St Christopher"* fresco on the wall above the door. The gigantic saint is shown crossing the lagoon with infant Jesus on his shoulder. The painting symbolically expresses the power of Venice. Through the door facing that of the Philosophers, we enter the living quarters of the Doge, which now house a painting collection. Among the paintings on exhibition are works by Hieronymus Bosch, Vittore Carpaccio, the Bassano family, as well as G.B. Tiepolo's famous *"Venice and Neptune"* in the Sala degli Scudieri (Room of the Squires). By way of the Golden Staircase, we reach the third floor also known as the second piano nobile and its halls filled with famous art works, luxurious decorations and furniture, all still in the places for which they were made. The highest officials of the Venetian Republic met in these rooms, and anyone admitted to these areas had to follow the strict protocol. The members of these committees were dignified and reserved, and they inspired fear and respect. A member of the Collegio reported that even the loquacious poet Francesco Petrarch's "voice trembled a little" upon addressing this intimidating group.

GOLDEN STAIRCASE

DOGE'S PRIVATE APARTMENT

Doges' Palace, Room of the Four Doors. Titian, Doge Antonio Grimani kneeling before Faith and St Mark in Glory.

Doges' Palace. The Golden Staircase.

Doges' Palace, the Golden Staircase. A Detail of the Stucco Decoration

CEILING

COUNCIL OF TEN HALL

Hall of the Council of Ten. Ceiling. Paolo Veronese. Juno, Queen of the Gods, Offering Venice the Doge's Cap.

NVNQVAM DERELIC. TA .

ROOM OF THE FOUR DOORS

The Square Drawing Room serves as the entrance to the second piano nobile. In the centre of the ceiling is *"Doge Girolamo Priuli Receiving the Scales and Sword from Justice"* by Jacopo Tintoretto and his assistants. The left door leads to a secret passageway to the Torture Room and the prisons. It was here that Casanova spent his last night in jail before his heroic escape across the roofs. Next is the Sala delle Quattro Porte

Room of the Four Doors.
The Arrival of Henry III King of France in Venice.
Andrea Vicentino (1593).

(Room of the Four Doors), a ceremonial ante-chamber for ambassadors waiting to be received by the Collegio, Senate and the Council of Ten. This room's important function is also revealed by its size, spanning as it does the width of the palace from the courtyard to the canal-side wall of the building. The paintings of historical and artistic significance include Titian's *"Doge Grimani before the Faith and St Mark in Glory"* (right wall), *"Jove Leading Venice to the Adriatic in Token of Domination over this Sea"* by Jacopo Tintoretto (ceiling fresco), and *"The Arrival of Henry III, King of France, in Venice in 1584"* by Andrea Vicentino (left wall). The Sala dell'Anticollegio and the Sala del Collegio were designed to repre-

ladio and Antonio Rusconi, with the stucco-work carried out by Marco del Moro. The Ante-chamber was embellished by Jacopo Tintoretto between 1577 and 1578, with masterpieces that include *"Mercury and the Graces,"* *"Vulcan's Forge"* *"Pallas Banishing Mars"* and *"The Discovery of Ariadne"*. In the period 1576-80, Paolo Veronese painted *"The Rape of Europa"* that today hangs in the same room, and in 1578 he made the

sent a Greek temple, with pronaos and sanctuary, in relation to their real functions. They are the Ante-chamber and Hall of the Collegio, the most exclusive governing body of the Republic. The architectural and decorative program of the Ante-chamber was designed in 1575 by Andrea Pal-

fresco *"Venice Conferring Rewards and Honours"* for the central section of the ceiling. The *"Return of Jacob"* by Jacopo da Ponte (il Bassano) is also found here.

ANTE-CHAMBER
AND HALL OF THE COLLEGIO

There is a sense of pomp and ceremony to the Hall of the Collegio which knows no equal in the other rooms of the Doges' Palace. The ceiling is sumptuously carved and gilded, and the walls embellished. The Doge's Throne and the numerous paintings complete the decorative program. The Hall was used primarily for meetings of the Consiglio Minore (Lower Council) and the Consiglio dei Savi (Council of the Sages). These meetings would be attended by the Doge and his advisers, the Head of the Council of Ten and the Great Councillor. Here, the Doge and officials would deliberate on the most important state problems in the utmost secrecy, and the decisions made would then be related to the bodies authorized to implement the plans. The Hall of the Collegio was also used to receive foreign princes and ambassadors, and for audiences given to procurators reporting back from missions and representatives from Venetian territories. The magnificent ceiling was carved by Francesco Bello and Andrea Faentin (1576), while the painting cycle was the work of Paolo Veronese. Veronese painted *"Neptune and Mars," "Faith"* and *"Venice Triumphant with Peace and Justice"* in the three central sections of the ceiling and allegories of the Virtues in the smaller surrounding frames. On the wall above the Doge's Throne is yet another masterpiece by Veronese, the *"Battle of Lepanto."*

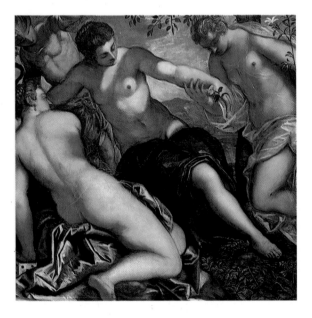

Hall of the College. Mercury and the Graces by J. Tintoretto.

Hall of the College. Allegory of the Battle of Lepanto by Veronese.

Vulcan's Forge by J. Tintoretto.

Pallas Banishing Mars by J. Tintoretto.

The Discovery of Ariadne by J. Tintoretto.

Doge Nicolò da Ponte Invokes the Virgin's Protection by J. Tintoretto.

PREGADI HALL OR SENATE. The gilded and carved ceiling in the Sala del Senato or dei Pregadi was made in 1582 by Cristoforo Sorte. Most of the painting cycle in this room was completed between 1581 and 1595 by Palma Giovane and Jacopo Tintoretto, and includes an interesting work by the latter, *"Doge Pietro Loredan Worshipping the Virgin."* The Sala del Consiglio dei Dieci (Hall of the Council of Ten) has always occupied a special place, even in the first Doges' Palace where it was isolated and accessible only by way of a special staircase from the ground floor. The Republic's Supreme Court of Law was held in this room. Paolo Veronese made the two ceiling paintings, *"Juno, Queen of the Gods, Offering Venice the Doge's Cap"* and *"Young and Old States"* the latter an allegory with an old man in a turban and a young woman. On the same floor we find the Sala della Bussola, Sala dei Capi del Consiglio dei Dieci (Room of the Heads of the Council of Ten), Inquisitors' Room, the Torture Room, and the Prisons. In the Hall of the Bussola, there is a *Bocca di Leone* (Lion's Mouth), which was a sort of mail box provided for secretly reporting crimes directly to the Council of Ten. In the Room of the Heads of the Council of Ten, there are paintings by Paolo Veronese, including *"Punishment of the Forger"* set in the ceiling. The small Inquisitor's Room has two paintings by Jacopo Tintoretto on the ceiling, *"Four Virtues"* and *"The Return of the Prodigal Son"*.

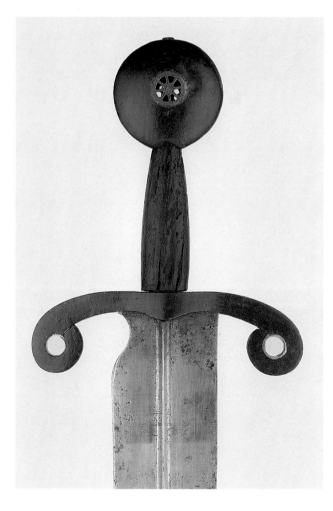

THE ARMOURY is located in the *Torresella* area of the prisons, where today (by asking the caretaker) one can see the very old graffiti and drawings left by some prisoners, and in the Stanza delle Armi del Consiglio dei Dieci (Armoury of the Council of Ten). The Council of Ten founded the armoury in the sixteenth century to defend the State after ongoing revolts, some even breaching the Doges' Palace itself. Recently, the Armoury has been reorganised. The original arms were added to over time by others left to the State by patrician families; gifts from visiting dignitaries and ambassadors were also kept here, as were entire collections of arms left by famous soldiers. Among the most interesting are the armour of Erasmo da Narni (known as the Gattamelata), an equestrian suit of armour of a Senator, and that of Henry IV, King of France. The collection comprises odd pieces including a pennon from a Turkish ship in the Battle of Lepanto, a bronze culverin by Alfonso Alberghetti, a harquebus from the seventeenth century, as well as assorted swords, pikes, harquebuses and musketoons. There is even an iron chastity belt, included perhaps as a reminder of ancient customs. From here we will descend the Scala dei Censori (Censors' Staircase) to the first piano nobile and proceed along the corridor which brings us to the Hall of the Quarantia Civil Vecchia and the Old Arms Room. In the rooms of the Quarantia Civil Vecchia members of the highest penal and civil magistrates held the Court of Appeals. On the walls of the Old Arms Room, there are burned and blackened fragments of the Paduan painter Guariento's fresco *"The Coronation of the Virgin,"* which originally occupied the wall above the Doge's Throne in the Hall of the Great Council, where Tintoretto's *"Paradise"* hangs today.

HALL OF THE GREAT COUNCIL

The Sala del Maggior Consiglio (Hall of the Great Council) measures: 54 x 25 x 15.4 metres, and is a singularly light-filled space due principally to its large windows set high up along the south wall giving onto the St Marks Basin. The Great Council was the legislative branch of the Venetian state and counted 1,600 members at the height of the Republic. Here they sat on wooden seats side by side in long rows occupying nearly all the space in the room. For special occasions like the visit of a prince, the seats were rearranged, and the room was used as a splendid reception hall. The ceiling panels and gilded frames were designed and carved by Cristoforo Sorte in 1582. Commissions for the ceiling paintings were given to Tintoretto, Veronese, Jacopo Palma il Giovane and Francesco Bassano, all of which were finished by 1584. The paintings on the walls were done between 1590 and 1600 by Tintoretto, Veronese and others. Jacopo Tintoretto's "Paradise" was hung in its present location in 1594. The following works occupy the central sections of ceiling and are concerned with the glorification of Venice: "Apotheosis of Venice" by Paolo Veronese (first), "Venice as Queen" by Jacopo Tintoretto (centre), and "Venice Crowned by Victory" by Jacopo Palma Giovane (third). There are three principle themes in the history paintings along the walls. On the right wall are episodes in the struggle between Emperor Frederick Barbarossa and Pope Alexander III and pertaining to the peace treaty negotiated by Doge Sebastiano Ziani (1172-78). The Fourth Crusade and the Conquest of Constantinople are narrated between the windows on the left wall. Along the wall facing the Doge's Throne is the War of Chioggia including Paolo Veronese's "Glorious Return of Doge Andrea Contarini and the Venetian Victory over the Genoese at Chioggia". The portraits of the first seventy-eight Doges are set below the ceiling.

Jacopo Tintoretto's "Paradise" is a painting made up of several different canvases that together reach a height of 7m and a width of 22m, the dimension of the entire short wall above the throne in the hall of the Great Council. The Senate had originally commissioned Paolo Veronese and Francesco da Ponte (il Bassano) to prepare sketches for this work, but upon Veronese's death in 1588, Tintoretto was summoned to take his place. Though the artist was already seventy years old, he went to work with his usual enthusiasm in the large room of the Confraternity of the Misericordia. During the two years required to complete the work, his son, Domenico, Jacopo Palma Giovane, and others provided him with the assistance he required. Once the work was completed the various sections were brought to the Doges' Palace and put in place. It received immediate admiration. The composition is centered around the figures of Christ and the Virgin surrounded by Angels, Saints and the Blessed. The light serves as a unifying element, giving the scene movement and life.

(p.90-91) Hall of the Senate. Detail of the central part of the ceiling.

(p.92) Hall of the Council of Ten. Paolo Veronese, Young and Old States.

(p.93) Venetian helmet covered in velvet with gilded copper and bronze decorations (late -15th century).

(p.93) Late-15th century sword.

(p.94-95) Hall of the Great Council. Paradise by Jacopo Tintoretto.

(p.96) Hall of the Great Council. Paolo Veronese, Apotheosis of Venice (detail).

(p.97) Hall of the Great Council. Apotheosis of Venice by Paolo Veronese.

Through a door at the west end of the Hall of the Great Council, we enter the Hall of the Quarantia Civil Nuova, the Court of Appeals for the inhabitants of the Republic's mainland territories. On the far wall hangs a large gilt leather ornament, one of the few remaining examples of the ancient tradition of the *Cuoridoro* that somehow escaped pillaging. The next room, the Sala del Scrutinio (Room of the Tally) played a vital role in the complicated elections of a new Doge and the elections for other state offices. The paintings in this room include portraits of the last forty-three Doges, below the ceiling, and other works pertaining mostly to the glorification of the Serenissima. These paintings are as follows: *"Last Judgment"* by Jacopo Palma Il Giovane (entrance wall), *"The Battle of Zara"* by Jacopo Tintoretto (right wall), *"The Battle of Lepanto"* by Andrea Vicentino (middle of right wall), and *"The Battle of the Dardanelles"* by Pietro Liberi (far end of right wall). The triumphs of Francesco Morosini are narrated in the Triumphal Arch framing the central doorway of the far wall. Morosini was the last famous commander of the Republican navy, who heroically reconquered historic Venetian strongholds in Morea and other territories taken by the Turks. Retracing our steps, past the Doge's Throne in the Hall of the Great Council and back through the Halls of Quarantia Criminale and the Court of Laws, we find the original marble Adam and Eve statues from the Foscari Arch by Antonio Rizzo. It is now time to cross the Bridge of Sighs and visit the Prisons. The famous Bridge of Sighs is a suspended passageway between the Doges' Palace and Prisons. The Prisons' walls are made of crudely finished massive blocks of stone, the windows are narrow and barred, and the doors are equipped with chains and bolts. This building reminds us of the legendary escape of Casanova from the lead-roofed attic cells, a favourite subject for nineteenth-century novelists and poets. The Bridge of Sighs is best seen from the Ponte della Paglia or ideally in a gondola passing below, because it is only from the exterior that one can possibly romanticize this bridge and forget its real and much more ominous function.

Torture Room.

Bridge of Sighs.

Prisons beyond the canal towards the St Mark's Basin.

THE ISLAND

OF SAN GIORGIO

"...nothing can compare with the space before Piazza San Marco. That vast mirror of water embraced by the half moon of Venice itself".

J.W. Goethe, Italian Journey

The island of San Giorgio is an ideal backdrop for the centre of Venice given its strategic position in the St Mark's Basin. Thus in defining the buildings and spaces of the Marciana area, the Venetian Republic obviously had a vested interest in the island and always strictly controlled the economic capacity of its institutions to be sure 'suitable' buildings would be constructed. In 982, the island was ceded to Giovanni Morosini, who founded a Benedictine monastery that received many privileges and donations. By 1178, at the death of Doge Sebastiano Ziani, the island had become a religious centre of European fame. An earthquake in 1223 damaged many of the buildings on the island, which were rebuilt under the auspices of Doge Pietro Ziani. The transformation of the island began in the early fifteenth century and continued, with brief interruptions, until the seventeenth century. Cosimo dei Medici, Lord of Florence, travelled to Venice in 1433 together with Michelozzi, who designed the Library in Renaissance style. In 1480, Buora designed an entire wing of the monastery comprising the friars' dormitories next to the friars' cells. The Cloister of the Bay Trees (1516-1540), the Abbots' Apartments and Chapter House (1553) and Longhena's replacement of Michelozzi's library were built. Between 1559-80 Andrea Palladio built the Refectory (1559-63), the Church of San Giorgio (1566-1610), and the Cloister of the Cypresses (1579-1614). The island is today home to the headquarters of the Giorgio Cini Foundation.

View of S.Giorgio from St Mark's campanile.

Grand Canal Regatta, 18th c. etching. Correr Museum, Venice.

THE GRAND CANAL

THE
STREET
OF THE ARISTOCRACY

THE PALACES

▢	L. Left.
▪	R. Right.
1	L. Dogana da Mar
1	R. Palazzo Contarini-Fasan
2	L. Bas. of S. Maria della Salute
3	L. Palazzo Dario
4	L. Palazzo Venier dei Leoni
2	R. Palazzo Corner della Ca' Grande
5	L. Palazzo Contarini dal Zaffo
3	R. Palazzi Barbaro
6	L. Palazzo Loredan dell'Ambasciatore.
4	R. Palazzo Grassi
7	L. Ca' Rezzonico
8	L. Palazzo Foscari
5	R. Palazzo Contarini dalle Figure
9	L. Palazzo Balbi
6	R. Palazzo Mocenigo
7	R. Palazzo Corner-Spinelli
10	L. Palazzo Bernardo
11	L. Palazzo Tiepolo
8	R. Palazzo Grimani
9	R. Palazzo Loredan
10	R. Palazzo Farsetti
11	R. Palazzo Manin
12	R. Fondaco dei Tedeschi
12	L. Palazzo Camerlenghi
13	R. Ca' da Mosto
14	R. Ca' d'Oro
13	L. Palazzo Corner della Regina
14	L. Palazzo Pesaro
15	L. Fondaco del Megio
15	R. Palazzo Vendramin-Calergi
16	R. Church of the Scalzi
16	L. Church of San Simeon Piccolo

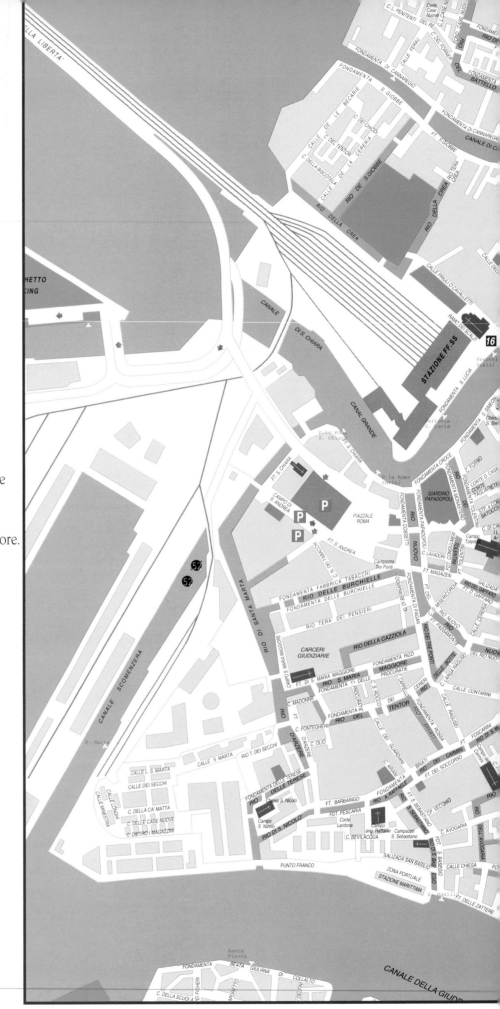

104

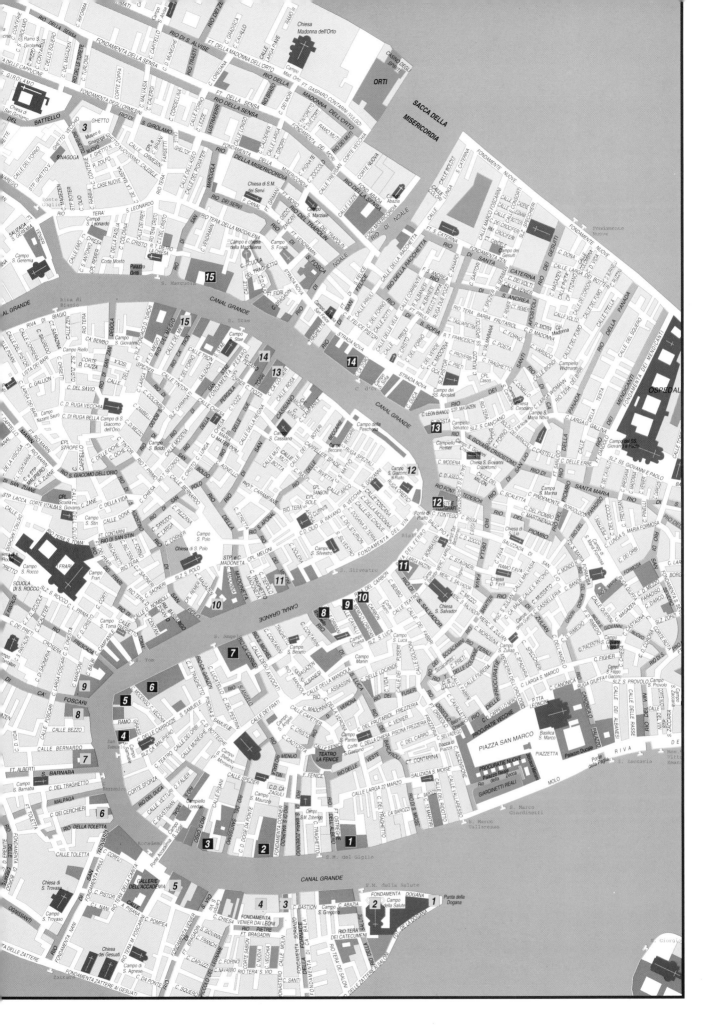

THE PALACES ALONG THE GRAND CANAL

LEFT BANK

DOGANA DA MAR

The Dogana da Mar, built around 1677 by the architect Giuseppe Benoni, has a distinctive tower topped with a large bronze sphere and a statue of Fortune. This was the site of the city's customs house through which all goods entering Venice from the sea passed from the beginning of the fourteenth century on.

SANTA MARIA DELLA SALUTE

The church was built by Baldassare Longhena between 1631 and 1681. The plan is octagonal and the church is raised high on a stepped pedestal. Pilasters and tympanums adorn the facades, and the church's large dome dominates the skyline.

RIGHT BANK

PALAZZO CONTARINI-FASAN

Palazzo Contarini-Fasan is in the Flamboyant Gothic style popular around 1475 with highly-decorated capitals and balconies. Some architectural and decorative elements foreshadow Renaissance taste. Legend has it that this was the house of Desdemona.

PALAZZO CORNER DELLA CA' GRANDE

Palazzo Corner della Ca' Grande was designed and built by Jacopo Sansovino between 1532 and 1565. The palace's three storeys are articulated on the facade by ashlar-work on the ground floor, three doorways to the atrium, and the projecting balconies.

PALAZZO TIEPOLO

This palace was built by the architect Gian Giacomo del Grigi in about 1560 for the Coccina family. It was later sold to the Tiepolos and then to the Papadopoli family. There have been many restorations, and a garden and extension to the building have since been added. It was famous for its collections of Veronese paintings, Murano glass, and coins, which have since been taken to various museums.

PALAZZO DEI CAMERLENGHI

This is a typical sixteenth-century Lombardesque building by Gugliemo dei Grigi. It was once the seat of the Exchequer, which commissioned Bonifacio Pitati and his workshop to decorate the interior with allegorical figures.

PALAZZO MANIN

Today the Banca d'Italia, the Classical style Palazzo Manin-Dolfin was the work of Jacopo Sansovino in the sixteenth century. The last Venetian Doge Lodovico Manin lived here.

FONDACO DEI TEDESCHI

This was built in the sixteenth century by the architects Giorgio Spavento and Antonio Abbondi, known as the "Scarpagnino." Giorgione decorated the facade with now-lost frescoes of nudes.

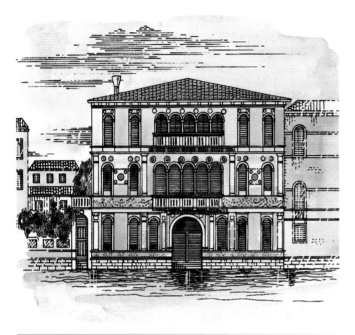

PALAZZO CONTARINI DAL ZAFFO

This building dates from the end of the fifteenth century and can boast of a noteworthy architectural and decorative balance. The architect is thought to have been Mauro Coducci who continued the work of Giovanni di Antonio Buora.

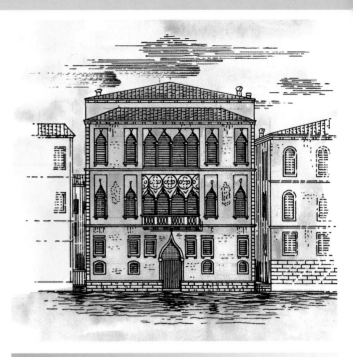

PALAZZO LOREDAN DELL' AMBASCIATORE

This is a Gothic building from the fifteenth century with arched windows and fifteenth-century niche statues. The house took its name from the fact that it became the Austrian Embassy in the eighteenth century.

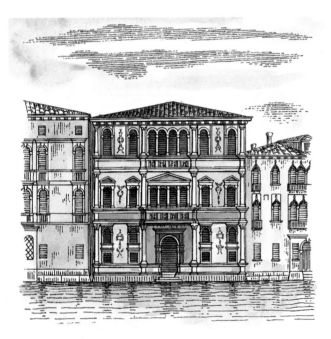

PALAZZO CONTARINI DALLE FIGURE

(Antonio Abbondi, known as the "Scarpagnino," 16th century). The building gets its name from the caryatids supporting the balcony. It is an early Renaissance construction and was the home of Palladio's patron, Jacopo Contarini.

PALAZZI MOCENIGO

This complex consists of four connected buildings with various Gothic and Renaissance elements. It was home to Lord Byron, Giordano Bruno, and Anne of Shrewsbury, whose love affair with Antonio Foscari caused him to be sentenced to death.

PALAZZO REZZONICO

(B. Longhena, 1667; G. Massari, 1750) Longhena's design, carried out by the Bon family, was completed only to the first storey. The Rezzonico family, who then bought the palace, hired Giorgio Massari to finish the work. He added the courtyard, grand staircase and ballroom (24 x 14 x 12 m).

PALAZZO FOSCARI

The sculptors Giovanni and Bartolomeo Bon built this as the home of Doge Francesco Foscari in 1452. It is one of the most impressive palaces on the Grand Canal, with its double piano nobile and elegant arch clusters on the facade, corresponding to the great halls inside. It is now the University of Venice.

PALAZZO CORNER SPINELLI

(Mauro Coducci, 15th-16th centuries). This is one of the noblest of Venetian palaces because of the balance of its parts and the innovative double balconies. It was remodelled by Sanmicheli in the sixteenth century.

PALAZZO GRIMANI

(Michele Sanmicheli, 16th century). This is a good example of Sanmicheli's mature architectural style, with the facade's three classical orders with columns and wide arches. It is a powerful structure which fully demonstrates the grandness and pomp of the Grimani family.

THE PALACES ALONG THE GRAND CANAL

LEFT BANK

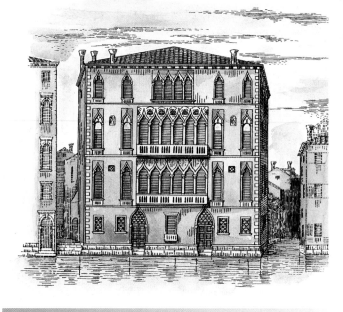

PALAZZO BALBI

This building includes some Renaissance elements, but ultimately has a decorative program typical of that popular in Venice at the end of the sixteenth century. It was designed by the architect and sculptor Alessandro Vittoria from Trent who was a frequent member of Venetian intellectual circles.

PALAZZO BERNARDO

The original architectural and decorative features of this mid-fifteenth-century Gothic palace are well-preserved. The Duke of Milan Francesco Sforza and his wife Bianca Visconti resided here as guests of the Republic in the mid-fifteenth century.

RIGHT BANK

PALAZZO LOREDAN

This is a Veneto-Byzantine style palace typical of the twelfth and thirteenth centuries. It was built for the Zane family, who later sold it to the Corners, who in their turn sold it to the Loredan family in the eighteenth century. Today it and the adjacent Palazzo Farsetti house the town hall.

PALAZZO FARSETTI

This palace was built in the twelfth century as a fondaco house and takes its name from the Tuscan family Farsetti who bought it in 1669. It was once the seat of the Accademia Farsetti, with its famous collection of plaster casts. The school was open to students, one of whom was Canova who did his training there. Today it is the site of the town hall.

PALAZZO DARIO

This early Renaissance building designed by the Lombardo family is rich with decorative motifs. The house is apparently cursed, and some of its owners, including the original owner Giovanni Dario and the Barbaros who bought it from Dario, have met with ill ends over the centuries.

PALAZZO VENIER DEI LEONI

This unfinished palace consists of an imposing ground floor and an ample garden, where the Venier family kept a lion, hence its name. Today it is home to the Peggy Guggenheim Collection of modern art.

PALAZZI BARBARO

One of the two adjacent Barbaro palaces was built in the seventeenth century and the other in Gothic style in the fifteenth century. They became the French Embassy, and in 1499 Isabella d'Este lived here. The buildings are luxuriously decorated with paintings and furnishings.

PALAZZO GRASSI

Giorgio Massari designed this Neoclassical palace in the eighteenth century. The arcaded courtyard, grand staircase and entire structure projecting itself toward the canal are all very powerful forms. A. Longhi's wall fresco above the staircase is of interest.

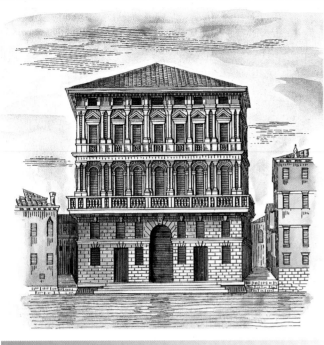

PALAZZO CORNER DELLA REGINA

This neoclassical palace was built in 1724 by architect Domenico Rossi for the Corner family on the site of an older palace, which had been the home of the Queen of Cyprus, Caterina Cornaro.

PALAZZO PESARO

This gigantic palace is the famous work of the architect Baldassare Longhena who lived to complete it to the first storey. It was finished by Antonio Gaspari. Today it houses the city's modern art museum.

CA' DA MOSTO

This thirteenth-century house shows the typical Veneto-Byzantine fenestration. It was once the grand hotel of the city, "Il Leon Bianco," where many famous people stayed, including the Counts of North in 1782.

CA' D'ORO

Matteo Raverti and the Bons built this for Marin Contarini between 1421 to 1440. The highly-decorated facade of this Gothic palace is well-known. Today it houses the Franchetti Collection.

FONDACO DEL MEGIO

This fifteenth-century building once contained the state granaries. The fortress-like walls are brick-faced with crenelations and loopholes.

CHIESA DI SAN SIMEON PICCOLO

This neoclassical church was built in the eighteenth century by G. Scalfurotto. The church is elevated on a high base, and its copper dome serves as a landmark in the railway station neighbourhood.

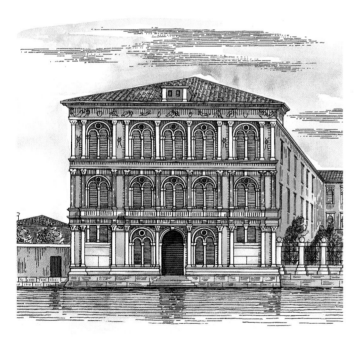

PALAZZO VENDRAMIN-CALERGI

This is one the most noble facades on the Grand Canal, with its perfectly balanced decoration and double-arch windows. It was begun by Mauro Coducci in 1504 and completed by the Lombardo workshop in 1509.

CHIESA DEGLI SCALZI

This church was designed by Baldassare Longhena in the seventeenth century and finished in the following century by Giuseppe Sardi, who added the Baroque facade. It has many interesting works of art including frescoes by G.B. Tiepolo and sculptures by Giovanni Marchiori.

THE RIALTO
BRIDGE

The Rialto Bridge is a Venetian landmark. It is
lined with shops, with their backs to the canal
and their windows facing the central staircase. To the right of the bridge is Palazzo Dol-
fin-Manin. Just beyond it, to the right, the
Fondaco dei Tedeschi is visible. On the opposite bank, to the left, is the foreshortened
Palazzo Camerlenghi.

VENICE CULTURE AND TRADITION

Marciana Library. Grimani Breviary, January.

It is difficult today to define what Venice's cultural heritage once was because of the political upheavals and wars that aided the foreign sale and/or appropriation of many masterpieces from patrician and middle-class families as well as religious and civic institutions. What we can see today is, in any case, an immense quantity of art works, church furnishings and devotional objects, whose sheer number can only make us wonder what has been lost. There are the following religious buildings: 5 abbeys, 213 churches, 31 cloisters, 70 convents and 64 guilds. They were all institutions to which the inhabitants would make donations and gifts. The palaces and houses of the upper classes also contained many works of art which represented an important part of the tradition of Venetian culture. Apart from what still remains in private hands, the art and historical collections are listed as follows: Sansoviniana Library, Accademia Galleries, Franchetti Gallery at Ca' d'Oro, Querini-Stampalia Gallery, Marciano Museum, Archaeological Museum, Pinacoteca Mantrediniana at the Seminario Patriarcale, Naval Museum at the Arsenale, Correr Museum, Risorgimento Museum, Collections of 18th century Venice at Cà Rezzonico, Museum of Modern Art at Cà Pesaro, Murano Glass Museum, Jewish Museum in the Ghetto, and the Peggy Guggenheim Collection of modern art in Palazzo Venier dei Leoni. The Sansoviniana Library is famous for antique bookbindings which date from the tenth to eighteenth centuries. The Accademia Galleries house the most important collection of Venetian art covering the early phases of the thirteenth and fourteenth centuries up until the eighteenth century, including the collections of Ascanio Molin (donated in 1815), Felicita Renier (in 1850), Gerolamo Contarini (in 1838) as well as recent acquisitions. In the Franchetti Gallery at Ca' d'Oro, paintings from the most important Italian schools are exhibited along with sculptures, bronzes,

Cà Rezzonico. Francesco Guardi, St Mark's Basin toward the Salute Church.

medals, furniture and tapestries. In the halls of the old Querini-Stampalia family residence at S.Maria Formosa, works from the Veneto and Venetian schools from the fourteenth to eighteenth centuries are hung: the gallery also has furniture, tapestries, ceramics, bronzes and coins on display. In the Marciano Museum, one finds the four original horses from the facade of St Mark's Basilica, which have been substituted with copies, as well as sacred vestments and fragments of ancient mosaics. The Archaeological Museum, which was based on Cardinal Domenico Grimani's bequest in 1523, possesses Roman copies of Greek statues, small statues, busts, Egyptian and Assyrian-Babylonian artifacts, and a numismatic collection. The Manfrediniana Gallery at the Seminario has architectural fragments, stone tablets and inscriptions from abolished churches and monasteries as well as paintings and busts. In the Naval Museum at the Arsenale there are models of ships and war trophies from the Napoleonic Era to the present. The Correr Museum, located in the Palazzo Reale in St Mark's Square, contains souvenirs of public life in the Serenissima and maps of Venice and the lagoon. The Risorgimento Museum shows evidence of life in Venice from the Fall of the Republic to the First World War. The 18th-century Museum in Ca' Rezzonico has eighteenth-century frescoes, paintings, and furnishings in period rooms. In Palazzo Pesaro on the Grand Canal, there are paintings and sculptures by modern Venetian, Italian and foreign artists. The Murano Glass Museum in Palazzo Giustiniani has a collection of glass objects that date from the fifteenth to nineteenth centuries. The Jewish Museum in the Ghetto displays cultic objects, vestments and traces of Jewish life, especially in Venice. The famous modern and contemporary art collection in Palazzo Venier dei Leoni on the Grand Canal was the work of Peggy Guggenheim, whose ashes are buried in the garden.

Accademia Galleries.
Vittore Carpaccio, the Legend of Ursula (detail).

Querini-Stampalia Gallery. Pietro Longhi, Duck Hunt.

117

THE
ACCADEMIA
GALLERIES

*The rooms of the Galleries are under restoration
and the location of the paintings is subject to change.
Our apologies.*

The Gothic church and ex-monastery of Santa Maria
della Carità is today the Fine Arts Academy, but from
the courtyard inside a section of the original building
by Palladio (1552) is visible. To the right is the Scuola
della Carità, once one of the city's six *scuole grandi*,
and today home to the Accademia Galleries, the city's
most important collection of art. Going up the eighteenth-century staircase, one arrives in the Sala del
Capitolo, whose gilt and inlaid wooden ceiling was
made in 1484 by the Vicentine artist Marco Cozzi.
There one find altarpieces and paintings with gold
backgrounds by fourteenth and fifteenth-century
Venetian masters working in the Veneto-Byzantine
and Gothic styles. The most interesting works in this
room are *"Polyptych with Saints and Scenes from the
Life of Christ and St Francis"* and *"Virgin and Child
Enthroned"* by Paolo Veneziano, Lorenzo Veneziano's
"Polyptych with the Annunciation and Saints" (1357),
"St James the Greater with Saints" and *"The Coronation of the Virgin"* by Michele Giambono (15th century), *"The Marriage of Santa Monica"* and *"The Virgin
and Child"* by Antonio Vivarini (15th century), and
two panel paintings by Jacobello del Fiore, *"The Coronation of the Virgin"* and *"Justice with Two Archan-
gels"* (1421).

In the second room there are works by Giovanni Bellini including *"Sacred Conversation"* and *"The Mourning of Christ."* There are also *"The Doubting Thomas"*
and *"The Virgin of the Orange Tree"* by Cima da
Conegliano. The third room contains paintings by fifteenth and sixteenth-century artists including Sebastiano del Piombo and Bernardino Licinio. In the
fourth room are three masterpieces of fifteenth-century Italian painting: Andrea Mantegna's *"St George"*
(1464), *"St Jerome"* by Piero della Francesca (mid-15th

century), and Cosmè Tura's *"Virgin and Child"*. There are paintings by Jacopo and Giovanni Bellini in the fourth and fifth rooms. In the fifth room are *"The Virgin of the Small Trees"* (1487) and the *"Pietà"* by Giovanni Bellini, and *"The Tempest"* by Giorgione (1505-07). This last painting represents an important period in the definition of style and composition in Venetian painting. In the sixth room are works by sixteenth-century painters including Bonifacio dei Pitati, Jacopo Tintoretto and Paris Bordone. Lorenzo Lotto's *"Portrait of a Gentleman in his Study"* hangs in the seventh room. There are paintings by Titian, Jacopo Tintoretto and Paolo Veronese in the tenth room. The oil paintings by Tintoretto are from the cycle he made for the Scuola di San Marco. They narrate the story of the life of the evangelist and include *"The Miracle of St Mark"* (1545-48). In this room is also Veronese's *"Supper in the House of Levi"* (1573), a painting that delights the viewer with its pleasing grandeur and rich sense of serenity which resonate from the open and classicizing architecture, the costumes of the figures and the quantity of details. In room eleven, there are many paintings by Veronese including his *"Marriage of St Catherine,"* *"Battle of Lepanto"* and *"Allegory of Venice"*. In the twelfth room are works by the eighteenth-century landscape artists Giuseppe Zais, Marco Ricci and Francesco Zuccarelli. Portraits by Tintoretto and works by Leandro and Jacopo Bassano hang in the thirteenth room. In room fourteen are seventeenth-century works by Domenico Fetti, Johann Liss and Bernardo Strozzi. Giambattista Tiepolo's *"Holy Family"* and *"St Gaetano"* are in the fifteenth room. In the sixteenth room is the famous painting by G.B. Piazzetta of a young sensual woman with a witty smile, *"The Fortune Teller"*. There are also portraits by Pietro and Alessandro Longhi here. The seventeenth room is divided into the following three areas: landscapes by Canaletto, Francesco Guardi, Michele Marieschi and Diziani; figure paintings by Sebastiano Ricci, G.B. Piazzetta, Jacopo Amigoni and G.B. Pittoni; and finally, Tiepolo's preparatory drawings for his ceiling fresco for the Church of the Scalzi, paintings by Pietro Longhi, and pastels by Rosalba Carriera. In room nineteen there are fifteenth and sixteenth-century paintings by Antonello da Saliba, Pietro da Messina and Vincenzo Catena. The twentieth room includes the *"Miracle of the Cross at San Lorenzo Bridge"* (1500) and *"Procession in St Mark's Square"* (1496) by Gentile Bellini, *"The Healing of the Madman"* by Vittore Carpaccio, and Giovanni Mansueti's *"Miracle in Campo San Lio"* and *" Miraculous Cure at San Polo"*. This last painting shows the interior of a fifteenth-century Venetian house. There is also Lazzaro Bastiani's *"Donation of a Relic of the Holy Cross to the Scuola di San Giovanni Evangelista"*. In room twenty-one, one finds Vittore Carpaccio's famous painting cycle for the Scuola di Sant'Orsola, which was founded in 1306 at the Church of Santi Giovanni e Paolo. Carpaccio is an able and imaginative narrator who documents Venetian interiors and depicts the members of that confraternity. Canvases by Bartolomeo Montagna, Giovanni and Gentile Bellini, Alvise Vivarini and Cima da Conegliano hang in room twenty-three. In the last room, called the Hostel Room, are *"The Presentation of the Virgin at the Temple"* by Titian (1538) and *"Virgin and Child Enthroned with the Doctors of the Church"* by Antonio Vivarini and Giovanni d'Alemagna.

(Pages 118-119) Vittore Carpaccio, the Legend of St Ursula.
The Arrival of the English Ambassadors.

Accademia Galleries, room XXI. Vittore Carpaccio, the Legend of St Ursula.
Ursula Welcomes Hereus and the Departure of the Pilgrims.

CA' REZZONICO

Palazzo Rezzonico, one of the most important buildings designed by Baldassare Longhena.

A view from the third floor window on the west side of Ca' Rezzonico, overlooking the San Barnaba Canal with the belltower of the Church of the Carmini in the background.

The construction of this palace was begun in 1667 by Baldassare Longhena for the Bon family, but only the first storey had been built at the time of the architect's death in 1682. Work was halted until the Rezzonico family bought the building and hired Giorgio Massari to complete it in 1750. Massari carried out Longhena's plans for the completion of the second storey, but he added his own designs for the courtyard, grand staircase and ballroom. This last space is grandiose (24 x 14 x 12m), spanning the entire width of the building.

CA' REZZONICO

MUSEUM OF EIGHTEENTH-CENTURY VENICE

The ceiling fresco in the ballroom was painted by G.B. Crosato around 1753 and depicts an allegory of the four parts of the world. The furniture was made by Antonio Brustolon (1700-23). The following room is known as the Room of the *Allegory of Marriage*, after G.B. Tiepolo's ceiling fresco. Among the people who lived in the mezzanine rooms on the ground floor are Clement XIII, the Rezzonico family and the poet Robert Browning, who died here in 1889. The Room of the Pastels takes its name from the series of pastel portraits by Rosalba Carriera. In the Tapestry Room, there are Flemish tapestries with scenes of Solomon and the Queen of Sheba. The Throne Room is famous for its 1758 ceiling fresco by G.B. Tiepolo, the *"Allegory of Merit between Nobility and Virtue"*. The golden throne was used by Pope Pius VI during his visit to Venice. In the Tiepolo Room, there is a ceiling painting done by Tiepolo between 1744 and 1745, as well as furniture from the Brustolon workshop. There is another set of Brustolon furniture in the room of the same name. The second floor gives a good idea of the intimacy of everyday living spaces in an eighteenth-century Venetian palace. In the Guardi Room are three frescoes by Francesco Guardi. The bedroom with the alcove shows a typical Venetian bed and two small lacquer side cabinets. The furniture is interesting and includes a bride's hope chest and a toilette set. In the Green Drawing Room, there are thirty pieces of green-gold lacquer Chinoiserie furniture, popular in the eighteenth century. On the wall, there is a curious painting of the lagoon iced over in 1788. The Longhi Room contains an important early ceiling painting by Tiepolo, *"The Triumph of Zephyr and Flora"*, and thirty-four small paintings by Pietro Longhi. These are part of the Longhi's amusing series of scenes of Venetians life. These paintings are rich in details and expressed with a particular wit. They include *"The Morning Chocolate"*, *"The Painter's Studio"*, *"The Toilette"*, *"Polenta"*, *"Horseback Ride"*, *"The Visit at the Convent"*, *"Family Concert Party"*, *"The Bautta"*, *The Furlana" "The Pharmacy"*, *"The Moor's Errand"*, *"The Essence Seller"*, and *"The Rhinoceros"*. In the Room of the Ridotto

Giorgio Massari's
18th-century ballroom at Ca' Rezzonico.

Cà Rezzonico.
The alcove with a painting of the Virgin by
Rosalba Carriera above the bed.

125

are two famous paintings by Guardi, *"Gaming Rooms"* and *"Nuns' Parlour"*, which depict members of the Venetian upper classes gathering at the San Moisè casino and in the nuns' sitting room at the Convent of San Zaccaria, where worldliness and religion came scandalously close in contact. Several small rooms follow in which period rooms from the villa of the Tiepolo family in Zianigo with frescoes by G.D. Tiepolo have been reconstructed. The better-known works from this villa include: *"Mondo Novo"* (dated 1791) which depicts a charlatan selling notions and advantages of a different society to the crowd at a country fair, *"Minuet at the Villa"* which shows an open-air country dance, and *"Three People Promenading"*. In the Room of the Clowns, the artist has portrayed a series of intriguing masked clowns, all dressed in white. These paintings include *"The Tumblers' House"*, *"Clowns Resting"* and the melancholy fresco *"Clown in Love"*. On the ceiling, clowns play in the fresco *"The Swing"*. On the third floor, there are numerous objects on exhibition, including collections of vases, chinoiserie, ceramics, costumes, drawings and the like. There is also an extremely interesting reconstruction of an antique pharmacy, complete with furnishings, jars, containers, a laboratory and stove, distiller, retorts and cruets. The Marionette Theatre contains original eighteenth-century marionettes which were part of that well-loved tradition in both Venetian theatres and private homes, as well as in the squares of the city.

G. Domenico Tiepolo,
The Clowns.

Pietro Longhi,
The Toilette;
Family Concert Party.

Francesco Guardi,
The Nuns' Parlour.

Pietro Longhi,
Fried Doughnut Seller.

Pietro Longhi,
Portrait of a Patrician Family.

127

The museum has a collection of works of nineteenth-century and twentieth-century Italian art as well as art from other countries. The nineteenth-century works include many Venetian artists and artists working in Venice and depict subjects of local interest. Some of the more important artists include Teodoro Matteini, Francesco Hayez, Ludovico Lipparini, Ippolito Caffi, Tranquillo Cremona, Federico Zandomeneghi; Gugliemo Ciardi, Giacomo Favretto, Luigi Nono, Alessandro Milesi, Pie-

CA' PESARO

MUSEUM OF MODERN ART

tro Fragiacomo, Ettore Tito; Giovanni Fattori, Telemaco Signorini, Giuseppe de Nittis, and Antonio Mancini. There are interesting sculptures by the twentieth-century artist Medardo Rosso as well as works by Umberto Boccioni, Gino Rossi, Arturo Martini, Felice Casorati, Pio Meneghini, Luigi Cadorin, Giorgio de Chirico, Carlo Carrà, Giorgio Morandi, Mario

Palazzo Pesaro.

Palazzo Pesaro. Museum of Modern Art.
Vittorio Zecchin, A Thousand and One Nights.

Palazzo Pesaro. Museum of Modern Art.
Head of a Boy by Medardo Rosso.

Sironi, Fillipo de Pisis, Massimo Campigli, Felice Carena, Virgilio Guidi, Bruno Saetti, Antonio Music, Mario de Luigi, Marco Novati, and Fioravante Seibezzi. There are also sculptors: Francesco Messina, Giacomo Manzù, Alberto Viani, Emilio Greco, and Claudio Trevi. The most famous foreign artists are Rodin, Limberman, Klinger, Marquet, Derain, Chagall, Matisse, Rouault, Klimt, Kandinsky, Klee, Grosz and Ernst.

CA' D'ORO

FRANCHETTI GALLERY

Ca' d'Oro is perhaps unique among Venetian Gothic buildings for its facade's elaborate decorative program with its composition of solids and voids, and its light traceried crowning, all in clear attempts to let air and light penetrate the facade wall. It is essentially a Gothic building with a particularly Eastern flair (built by Matteo Raverti and the Bon brothers, 1421-40). Today Ca' d'Oro houses the collection of Baron Giorgio Franchetti which includes the following: marble busts of the Procurators of St Mark's by Alessandro Vittoria, a marble lunette by Jacopo Sansovino, Carpaccio's *"Annunciation"* and *"Transit of the Virgin"*. A *"Venus"* by Titian, Andrea Mantegna's *"St Sebastian"*, *"The Queen of Sheba and Solomon"* by Francesco da Ponte il Bassano, and Van Dyck's *"Portrait of a Knight"*.

Cà d'Oro.

Franchetti Gallery. The Piazzetta by Francesco Guardi.

Franchetti Gallery. St Sebastian by Andrea Mantegna.

Franchetti Gallery. Battle of Satyrs and Giants,

by Vittore Gambello.

The Jewish Museum. 18th-century Venetian Jews
(from a painting depicting the circumcision ceremony (Milah).

Bridge and houses in the Ghetto Nuovissimo.

The Jewish Museum. Ornament for law scrolls (rimmon),
Venetian, late-17th century.

Jews of German origin were first permitted to settle permanently in Venice after the Republic, then in financial straits, granted them permission to lend money with interest following the War of Chioggia (1378-80). The Ghetto dates back to 1516 when Jews who had been living in outlying parts of the city and mainland were forced to move here and therefore remain segregated from the rest of the city's population. After the Germans, waves of Italian, Levantine, Spanish and Marrano Jews settled here. Jews were not allowed to leave the Ghetto and live in other parts of the city until 1797. During the centuries of segregation, the Jews were able to maintain a sort of separate state with their own traditions, temples and schools. The Ghetto comprises these three parts: Ghetto Vecchio (1541), Ghetto Nuovo (1516) and Ghetto Nuovissimo (1633). The synagogues include the following: Scola Spagnola (by Baldassare Longhena, 17th century), Scola Levantina (1538), Scola Italiana (1575), Scola Canton (1531-32) and Scola Grande Tedesca (1529).

The Jewish Museum has many traditional objects of the Jewish cult on exhibition. Visiting the synagogues and Jewish Museum is interesting even for non-Jews because these places serve to document the culture of a community that made a contribution to the history of Venice.

*Ghetto Vecchio.
Calle of the old Ghetto
looking towards
Cannaregio.*

*Ghetto Nuovo.
Houses on the Rio of
the new Ghetto looking
towards Ghetto
Nuovissimo.*

THE SCUOLE GRANDI

Jacopo Tintoretto, *Purloining the Body of St Mark.*
Once in the Scuola Grande of St Mark, now in the
Accademia Galleries.

*T*he scuole were religious associations dedicated principally to works of charity in times of need, famine, plague, and war. They were guild-like organizations that kept the books of law which listed the rules of the various trades; and they were also the patrons of various arts and crafts. Other scuole were founded by foreigners and were dedicated to assisting their fellow countrymen who were living in or visiting Venice. The scuole grandi included Santa Maria della Carità, the Misericordia, San Giovanni Evangelista, San Marco, San Rocco, San Teodoro and were nearly all founded in the mid-fourteenth century, being heavily influenced by the Franciscan and Dominican Orders.

The devotional confraternities also took the name *battuti* (flagellants) and would flail themselves during processions. At first, all citizens were allowed to be members of the scuole, but as time passed the patricians were prohibited from socializing with other social classes. The middle class, therefore, populated these bodies and carried out charges including Guardian Grando, Guardian de Matin and the Banca, which together were responsible for the management of the administration. After the fall of the Republic and the arrival of Napoleon, many of the possessions and buildings owned by the scuole were confiscated. Venice was deprived of a great deal of her innumerous works of art. Objects taken from the scuole were generally put into museums in Milan and Venice or taken out of the country. The Scuola Grande di San Rocco was the only one able to avoid this pillaging and keep its artistic patrimony and building intact. The famous paintings of the Miracles of the Cross were taken from the Scuola Grande di San Giovanni Evangelista and put in the Accademia Galleries, as were the paintings of the Miracles of St Mark from the Scuola Grande di San Marco.

Vittore Carpaccio. Legend of St Ursula. The Arrival of the English Ambassadors at the Court of the King of Brittany. Once in the Oratory of the scuola di S.Orsola at Ss Giovanni e Paolo, now in the Accademia Galleries.

135

THE JESUS
OF SAN ROCCO

SCUOLA GRANDE DI SAN ROCCO

Querini Stampalia Painting Gallery, Venice. G. Bella. The Doge's visit to San Rocco.

The construction of the Scuola Grande di San Rocco was first begun in 1515, under Antonio Abbondi known as "Scarpagnino," and from 1560 until completion, under Giangiacomo dei Grigi. The building has two large rooms on the first and second floors, with service areas and rooms on the right side, and two large staircases that meet halfway up to the luxurious and refined upper floor. The Scuola owes its fame to the painting cycle Jacopo Tintoretto made here in the twenty-four years between 1564 and 1588. The artist first painted the large canvases on the walls of the Great Upper Hall which depict the Life of Christ including the "Adoration of the Shepherds", "The Baptism", "Resurrection", "Prayer in the Garden", "The Resurrection of Lazarus", "The Ascension", "Christ Heals the Paralytic", and "Christ Tempted by Satan". The paintings on the ceiling relate the following stories from the Old Testament: "Moses Strikes Water from the Rock", "Adam and Eve", "God Appears to Moses", "Jonah Emerges from the Whale", "The Miracle of the Bronze Serpent", "The Vision of Prophet Ezekiel", "Jacob's Ladder", "The Sacrifice of Isaac", "The Fall of Manna in the Desert", "Elijah is Fed by the Angel", "Elisha Distributes Bread" and "Passover".

HOSTEL
UPPER HALL

GROUND FLOOR HALL

In the middle of the ceiling in the Hostel Hall is *"St Rocco in Glory,"* the painting which secured Tintoretto's commission to decorate the interior. He donated it, a finished oil painting, to the *scuola* and won the competition hands down as the others had submitted only drawings. For the wall facing the entrance in this room, Tintoretto painted an immense *"Crucifixion"* whose triangular composition emphasizes the central Christ figure. The other canvases here are *"The Ascent to Calvary"* and *"Christ before Pontius Pilate,"* in which Christ, wrapped in a white robe, stands alone and seemingly untouchable above an anonymous crowd. Two famous works by Titian were brought here from the Church of San Rocco, *"Christ Carrying the Cross"* and *"Dead Christ",* which stand on easels. Returning to the Great Hall, one can view Titian's *"Annunciation",* Tintoretto's *"Visitation",* and G.B. Tiepolo's *"Abraham and the Angels"* and *"Hagar Abandoned",* which are displayed at the other end of the room. By descending the great staircase, the first part of whose walls are covered with seventeenth-century paintings, one can admire more of Tintoretto's works downstairs relating to the New Testament, including the *"Annunciation", "Adoration of the Magi", "Flight into Egypt", "Slaughter of the Innocents","St Mary Magdalene", "St Mary of Egypt", "Circumcision"* and *"Assumption".*

Ground floor hall. Jacopo Tintoretto, Flight into Egypt.
Upper hall, ceiling. Jacopo Tintoretto, Original Sin.
Hostel Hall. Jacopo Tintoretto, Spring.

143

Ground floor hall. Jacopo Tintoretto, St Mary of Egypt.

Ground floor hall. Jacopo Tintoretto, Nativity (detail).

Hostel hall, ceiling. Jacopo Tintoretto, Autumn.

Tintoretto was born Jacopo Robusti in Venice in 1519, and lived here until his death in 1594. He was the son of a dyer, called *tintore* in Italian, which is where his nickname comes from. His training as a painter is not clear except for a period in the workshop of Titian, which he was apparently asked to leave because the master did not appreciate Tintoretto's painting style. However, it seems that Tintoretto's own workshop bore a sign reading "Drawing of Michelangelo and Colour of Titian". It can be said that Tintoretto knew the paintings of the great masters of the Renaissance well, and that in the works at San Rocco he had decided to leave them behind, forging ahead with a style all his own. The gigantic figures of the common people who crowd his paintings owe something to Michelangelo. Light is ultimately the most important element for Tintoretto as he used it to highlight the colours and unify his angular, action-filled compositions.

VENETIAN HOLIDAYS

Procession the night before Good Friday.

Palm Sunday, G.Bella.
Querini-Stampalia Gallery, Venice.

One could say that Venice is always ready for a holiday, and, in the past, official celebrations to commemorate any historical event of importance to Venetian life would continue even after centuries had passed. This also happened for events of more limited interest like the patron saint's day or a nobleman's wedding. The oldest Venetian holiday was that of the Feast of the Marys, which served to commemorate the city's victory over the pirates who had robbed the Venetians of their brides and their dowries from the church of San Pietro in Castello.

To honour those who had shown valour in chasing the pirates to Caorle and finally defeating them were mostly the tradesmen known as casselleri, who made hope chests for the brides and who had their workshops in the parish of Santa Maria Formosa. On the anniversary of the victory, the Doge would visit their church, and as time passed the celebrations would be accompanied by music and wine and great sums were spent. In 1379, at the time of the Invasion of Chioggia, the Feast of the Marys was abolished due to the difficult economic conditions of the population. The holiday Giovedì Grasso (Thursday before Shrove Tuesday) commemorated the struggle of the Bishop of Grado upheld by Venice against Ulric, the Bishop of Aquileia, who was defeated and taken prisoner. The Pope intervened and Ulric was freed on the condition that every year he would send a bull and twelve pigs, which symbolized the Patriarch and his twelve canons. On Giovedì Grasso the bull and pigs were slaughtered in St Mark's Square in the presence of the Doge and the Signoria, with the crowds looking on. This was celebrated until the sixteenth century, when it was abolished so as not to offend Friuli, which had been annexed by the Republic. Good Friday was traditionally the gravest day of

Holy Week. The Doge, Signoria and the members of all the Venetian Scuole Grandi, dressed in black, would take part in a long night-time procession. This holiday had a tragic character and once the procession had ended in St Mark's the penitent marchers would continue on through the numerous parishes of the city. Another feast day marked the visit of the Doge to the monastery of San Zaccaria, where the richly endowed daughters of Venetian nobility who were not to be married once spent their lives. In the parade which preceded the Doge, a page carried a silver basin with a corno (cap) the Doge had received as a gift. Scenes of these holidays were popular subjects for eighteenth-century painters, during that age of decadence when the nuns at San Zaccaria and other convents were rather well-known for much less spiritual reasons. The Sensa or Marriage to the Sea marked the victory over the pirates of the Narenta and was celebrated with a procession of boats that accompanied the Doge's Bucentaur to the Church of San Nicolò on the Lido where the Doge would cast a ring into the lagoon, in a symbolic marriage to the sea. There were also the Feast of the Corpus Domini and the Feast of the Redentore (Redeemer). The latter is still observed today (on the third Sunday of July) to commemorate the end of the plague in 1575. The Redentore is celebrated primarily at night with feasts in boats, which then sail to the Lido to see the sunrise. The Doge's annual visit to San Rocco was also to celebrate the anniversary of the end of the plague in 1575. He was received by the members of the scuola and attended high mass there. On November 21, instead, is the Feast of the Salute (Health), when the Doge gave thanks for the end of the plague in 1630. The Feasts of the Salute and the Redentore and the Historic Regatta are still Venetian holidays today.

The Doge's visit to San Zaccaria. Copy by A. Canal. Correr Museum, Venice.

The Bucentaur with a procession of boats at S.Nicolò. G.Bella. Querini-Stampalia Gallery, Venice.

THE
REGATA STORICA

Regata Storica. The boat procession in the Grand Canal at the Rialto Bridge.

Regata Storica. The boat procession in the Grand Canal in front of the Church of the Salute.

Regata Storica. The boat procession in St Mark's Basin.

Regata Storica. One of the historical boats preceding that of the Doge.

The Regata Storica (Historical Regatta), a race of two-man *gondolini*, is a famous holiday which has been celebrated down the centuries with much official pomp and a great enthusiasm among Venetians and foreigners alike. The Grand Canal lends itself naturally as a spectacular site for this regatta, which has been perfected over the years and become ever more popular. The event itself was made more interesting by the inclusion of official ceremonies before the race. The actual race was pre-ceded by a parade of *bissone* vessels with many oarsmen. Like Carnival floats, these boats were decorated with symbolic and allegorical marine figures on the prows and sterns and filled with people in fancy dress. The Doge himself, from high on the prow of his own large boat, would parade down the Grand Canal, waving to the enormous number of spectators who were crowded on every boat and dock available as well as those looking on from the windows and even the roofs of the palaces

148

facing the canal. The regatta ends in front of Ca' Foscari, where the doge personally awarded the winner a pig as first prize. Even if the two-man gondolino was the traditional boat for this regatta, other types of boats (which today are raced in individual heats) were allowed, and the celebrations went on in the evenings with feasts and fire-work displays.

CARNIVAL
IN VENICE

This is not the place to describe in great detail the Venetian Carnival, well-known across Europe in the eighteenth century and equally famous today as a historical celebration. Its festivity is well-documented in period prints, paintings and literary descriptions.

In the eighteenth century Venice had a very particular way of celebrating Carnival that involved rich and poor alike, not only the nobility and foreigners, both of whom were many, but all the inhabitants of Venice. Feasts were held city-wide. In nearly every square, from Dorsoduro to Castello, from Cannaregio to Santa Croce, there were festivities and theatrical or musical events, with the most important celebrations naturally in St Mark's Square. At first, these were open-air dances with some accompanying musicians playing violins and cellos or flutes and drums, followed by improvised buffet dinners on long tables lit by candles inside coloured balls. Dancing was even permitted in the squares near monasteries, but only until sunset. From the mid-thirteenth century the use of masks that completely concealed one's identity were allowed during Carnival. This concession by the state met a particular need or rather request by the citizens who wanted to indulge in frenzied cheer and various amusements with no threat of recognition. (The Republic, at one point, did attempt to limit and prohibit the use of masks, but failed in its effort and eventually gave up.) Many works of art, especially from the eighteenth-century, document the grandness of the festivities organized by the Republic and processions of the *scuole* and trade guilds on Giovedì Grasso and the last day of Carnival. These reproductions show the grandstands and galleries built to accommodate the hordes of spectators, the many participants and the processions of masked frolickers who dance, sing and play as the spectators look on. Other events at St Mark's included bull fighting, a Turk's tight-rope walk across a double cord from the Campanile to the roof of the Doges' Palace, the tasks of Hercules, all of which were repeated in other squares around the city or on boats in wider canals on following days. There were also fire-work displays. The Doge and members of the Signoria were always present in the most sumptuous of their fancy dress.

Multi-coloured masks and a group in costume at today's carnival.

150

THE FEASTS
OF THE REDENTORE

AND OF THE SALUTE

The Boat Procession for the Redentore.
G.Heintz. Correr Museum, Venice.

The Feast of the Redentore (Redeemer) is still celebrated on the third Sunday of July by large numbers of people who gather by day in front of the church of the Redentore on the Giudecca, which is connected to the Zattere by a bridge of barges across the Giudecca Canal assembled for this special occasion. At night, the festivities continue with people eating and drinking in the many boats which crowd the canal and on all along the docks, to witness the spectacular fireworks display. It is tradition to then go on to the Lido to watch the sun come up. This is an occasion to seek relief from the summer heat, because by staying for hours on end in boats, one is left with a healthy, refreshed feeling. Of course the preparations, which go on for days, also help cheer everyone up. It has always been a part of Venetian culture to spend time together with friends, chatting and gossiping about unimportant things, drinking wine and singing traditional songs like *"St Mark and his Lion"*, and reminiscing about times gone by, about the city's glorious past which speaks directly from the stones of its buildings into the hearts and souls of today's inhabitants.

The "foghi" or fireworks for the Redentore.

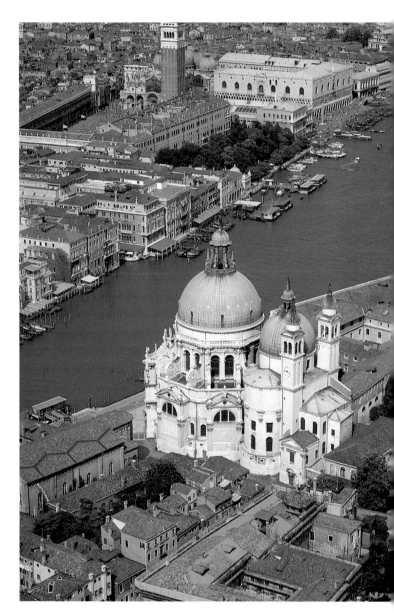

The Basilica of Santa Maria della Salute.

One of Venice's most striking architectural masterpieces is the Church of Santa Maria della Salute, which owes its founding to a decree of the Senate of the Republic on October 22, 1630 as a temple to the Virgin Mary in thanks for the end of the plague. The Feast of the Salute has been celebrated every November 21st from the time the church was completed in 1681. On that day, practically every inhabitant of Venice and the nearby mainland towns makes a pilgrimage to the Salute to ask the Virgin's blessing for good health. A wooden bridge supported by barges is built across the Grand Canal in front of Santa Maria del Giglio to allow people to cross over to the church and visit the many stalls where religious items are sold next to the steps of the church. All day long, crowds of people pour into the church and bow down in front of the image of the Virgin. And after they have said their prayers, they socialize with friends, perhaps exchanging wishes for continued good health across the tables of some favourite restaurant. The Feast of the Salute was once a much more elaborate affair, with the Doge and Signoria parading to the Salute with great pomp and ceremony and attending a high mass with official proceedings and the like. Today the holiday has maintained that sense of a gathering together of people united by an almost universal, if perhaps unconscious, religious sentiment.

MONASTERIES

The cloisters of the monastery of
Santa Maria dei Frari.

S.Francesco della Vigna Cloister.

The monasteries, abbeys and convents played a prominent role in the city's religious and social life. For the influence they exercised and the works of art which they contained, it is important to remember at least some of the names: the Camaldolese Abbey at San Michele in Isola, now the city cemetery, with its interesting facade designed by Mauro Coducci; the Abbey of the Misericordia with its church and scuola grande; the Abbey of San Cipriano in Murano; the Abbey of San Gregorio, which was particularly powerful in the thirteenth century when the monks moved there from the Abbey of Sant'Ilario on the edge of the lagoon in an area which had become unsafe due to battles between the Venetians and Paduans. Of this last abbey, the church, a small courtyard and the water gate with its large relief of St Gregory are still visible from the Grand Canal. The Convent of the Canonical Laterans at the Carità was transformed into the Academy of Fine Arts and the Accademia Galleries. Other convents included Santa Maria

Island of S. Giorgio. The Cloister of the Cypresses.

della Celestia, the Dominican Convent at Santi Giovanni e Paolo, the Convent of Santa Maria della Fava, the Franciscan convent at Santa Maria dei Frari, and the Gesuati and Gesuiti convents, the Maddalena on the Giudecca, the Madonna dell'Orto, Santa Maria dei Miracoli, Ognissanti, the Capuchin Friars at the Redentore, San Cipriano, San Francesco della Vigna, San Giorgio Maggiore, San Sebastiano, the Scalzi and the Templars. In some cases, only the place names survive of these religious institutions that were so full of works of art, altarpieces and sacred hangings. After the fall of the Serenissima Republic, which had attempted to give order to and regulate these religious societies, most of these institutions were closed or transformed and their artistic riches dispersed. Two of these centres, Santa Maria dei Frari and Santi Giovanni e Paolo, are now active. The amount of land and the quantity of works of art these two still own gives a good idea of the importance these monasteries once had.

St Apollonia Cloister.

THE BASILICA OF
SANTA MARIA GLORIOSA

DEI FRARI

The Basilica of Santa Maria of the Frari is an architectural element of the former monastic complex comprising two cloisters, the cells of the Franciscan monks and rooms for meetings and prayer. The complex as we see it today dates to the fourteenth, fifteenth and sixteenth centuries. The church is now visited by a large number of people, both for its architectural interest, in that its Gothic forms are punctuated by wide rhythms in both a horizontal and a vertical sense, and for its rich patrimony of works of art. Foremost among them are Titian's *"Assumption of the Virgin"* and the Pesaro Madonna, Giovanni Bellini exquisite triptych, Donatello's St John the Baptist, a triptych by Bartolomeo Vivarini, the Monument to Doge Tron by Antonio Rizzo and a statue of John the Baptist by Jacopo Sansovino.

Basilica of Santa Maria of the Frari.
The interior with the choir and the Assumption of the Virgin
by Titian in the background.

Basilica of Santa Maria of the Frari.

Basilica of Santa Maria of the Frari. High altar.
Titian. The Assumption of the Virgin.

THE *BASILICA* OF *SANTI GIOVANNI* E *PAOLO*

Campo Santi Giovanni e Paolo.
Scuola Grande di San Marco.
The Canal and the Bridge before the Campo.

Campiello Querini-Stampalia.

Campo Santi Giovanni e Paolo.
The Scuola, the Basilica and the Monument.

Campo Santi Giovanni e Paolo.
Andrea Verrocchio, Equestrian statue of
Bartolomeo Colleoni.

SS. Giovanni e Paolo is the name of a noted monastic complex of the Dominican order, at the north-east of the city. The complex comprised the church, cloisters, gardens and meeting and prayer rooms. The Dominicans today perform services in the church, and the cloisters, gardens and conventual buildings have been given over to the city hospital, together with the buildings of the former Scuola di San Marco, adjacent to the church. Since the 13th century, when the order received land to build on in the area from Doge Jacopo Tiepolo, SS. Giovanni e Paolo increased continually in importance and prestige. The church early became a burial-place for many Doges and was enriched with prestigious works of art and funeral monuments, and as in many other parts of Italy and Europe became the "opposite number" of the Franciscan church of the Frari. The view from the square outside already provides a strong sense of beauty and majesty, with the simple pedestal of the extremely powerful figure of the mercenary general, Colleoni exemplifying courage and strength; the facade of the Scuola di San Marco with its sculptures and beautiful marbles, provides a note of refined elegance. The interior of the church repeats the movement of the Frari church, but is lighter thanks to the southern orientation of the apse. The most noteworthy works of art include a polyptych by G. Bellini, canvases by G.B. Piazzetta and P. Veronese, and the numerous funeral monuments ranged along the walls.

MINOR VENICE

When people talk or write about Minor Venice, they mean those places off-the-beaten track, far from the usual thoroughfares such as the Mercerie, Rialto Bridge, Strada Nuova, Grand Canal, St Mark's Basin or the Giudecca Canal. It goes without saying that these out-of-the-way places are of no less importance than those of the "official" Venice. The canals, bridges, and squares of this "other" Venice have their own particular charm with gondolas gliding by, reflections on the water, people sitting on the sides of the streets taking notes or sketching, or countless other scenes of everyday life. This other Venice is the actual urban fabric of Venice, which is shaped by small canals and streets so narrow that it is sometimes difficult to get by. It is characterized by low buildings allowing one to occasionally glimpse a bit of the sky above, by people gossiping in the streets or even from one window to another overhead, by the sudden tolling of bells, or even by the tourists who pay homage to this city in their own particular way. It is best to wander around a bit, down the streets and along the canals without a precise destination, because just when you least expect it, some Gothic palace, some square with its monument, some facade or apse-end of a church, or some marble sculpture will unexpectedly catch your eye. For example, walking down the Calle dell'Olio to San Giovanni Evangelista, one is pleasantly surprised by the sight of a delightful Renaissance sculpted arch. Or, when coming from the Station or Piazzale Roma towards the San Tomà water-bus stop, you walk along the heavily-trafficked thoroughfare of Campo San Rocco where, if you are not careful, you could miss the massive, white Istrian stone, Renaissance facade of the Scuola Grande di San Rocco, the building of the Scoletta next to the Church of San Rocco, and the spectacular apse-end of the Church of Santa Maria Gloriosa dei Frari. It is worth visiting the Scuola Grande di San Rocco in order to view its grand halls filled with carved wooden wainscots and about forty paintings by Jacopo Tintoretto. The Scuola Grande di San Rocco is a reference point for Tintoretto's work and is visited by nearly all tourists. A bit further down the street, you come to Campo San Tomà with its low houses, where you should note the sculpture above the doorway (1478) of the Scuola dei Calegheri, the square's charming well-head, and the facade of the Church of San Tomà with its truncated belltower. Going on towards the Rialto, you pass Palazzo Centani, where Carlo Goldoni was born, and then come to the Church of San Polo, with its belltower and the vast square behind the church. Between Calle della Madoneta and Calle delle Erbe, there is an interesting building with a fifteenth-century Lombardesque mullioned window on the corner. After Campo San Aponal, one comes to the neighbourhood of the Rialto Markets. It is possible to find just about anything there, from fruit and vegetables to fish, cheese, oil, or any sort of alcoholic beverage, as well as the famous cicheti (traditional Venetian snacks) that are sold in the numerous trattorias there. History is most evident in the street names. We are reminded of Shylock who rented the galleys for the Levant, the noblemen who were money-changers, Carpaccio's paintings of the first wooden Rialto Bridge, the traffic between the Grand Canal banks, the palace of the Patriarchs of Grado (of which a cornice remains, visible on the other side of the Grand Canal, from the Riva del Carbon). Here are Ruga degli Orefici (Goldsmiths' Street), Porticato of the Campogiro, and the areas known as the Erbaria (fruit and vegetable market), Pescaria (fish Market), Beccaria (meat market), Panetteria (bread market), and that of the Botteri (cask makers). The Rialto is traditionally considered the oldest part of Venice. There is an oratory here which was founded in the fifth century. The history of the place is evident everywhere here, in the dark porticoes, in the narrow streets, and even in the ways and customs of the people who live there today. Moving along to Campo Santa Maria Mater Domini, you find yourself in a fourteenth-century square. Another interesting route - well what isn't in this city? - starts at San Giovanni Crisostomo, and goes on to the external staircase at the Palazzi Morosini, then the Corte del Milion to the house of Marco Polo, who wrote a book, "Il Milione", about his incredible thirteenth-century journeys to the East. Another very important area includes the Church of Santi Giovanni e Paolo and its square with the equestrian statue of Bartolomeo Colleoni and the facade of the Scuola di San Marco. Corte Bottera, which is adjacent to this square is also very interesting. In the Scuola di San Giorgio degli Schiavoni is a series of paintings by Vittore Carpaccio. The Ghetto is crowded with houses, some reaching eight storeys. The Ghetto took its name from the foundries there, where the Republic would gettare (or cast) metal for cannons. The Jews were first segregated in that area in 1527. At Santa Fosca, it is important to remember Fra Paolo Sarpi who supported the rights of the Serenissima in the period of the Interdict pronounced by Pope Paul V against Venice in 1606. These are just some of the many walks one can take to appreciate the thousand faces of this unfathomable city.

FROM
TEATRO *LA FENICE*

TO *CAMPO SAN LUCA*

The area stretching from St Mark's Square, to Campo San Stefano, Campo San Luca and beyond up to the foot of the Rialto Bridge includes the following points of interest: La Fenice Opera House, the Contarini del Bovolo's external spiral staircase, Campo San Stefano, Campo Sant'Angelo with Palazzo Duodo (no. 3584) where the composer Cimarosa lived and died, Campo San Benedetto dominated by Palazzo Fortuny whose windows look directly onto the church. La Fenice is a jewel of a building with modest dimensions, built by Antonio Selva in the eighteenth century. The theatre was destroyed in a fire in 1996 and rebuilt in 2003. In Campo Santo Stefano there are the Morosini,

Pisani, and Loredan Palaces and the Church of Santo Stefano, which has many works of art as well as the tomb of Francesco Morosini, known as the Peloponnesian. In the nearby Piscina San Samuele is the house of Paolo Veronese and Titian, Tullio Lombardo and others once had their workshops here. The district was known for its stories of adultery and forbidden loves. Pietro Aretino is buried in the Church of San Luca.

Sant'Andrea
Canal and Bridge.

Teatro La Fenice.

Rio di San Trovaso.

Palazzo Contarini
del Bovolo. Spiral staircase.

Rialto Market and Facade of
San Giacometto di Rialto.

The Renaissance Church of San Giovanni Crisostomo was built Mauro Coducci in the late-fifteenth century. The small Corte del Milion, behind the church, preserves fragments of Byzantine buildings from the eleventh and twelfth century. The name is derived from the houses that Marco Polo's family owned here, and the name of his book where he told the story of his journeys to the Orient and his encounters with the Gran Mogul (1271-1275). Campo Santi Giovanni e Paolo is an extremely interesting centre for its art and tradition. The church is a sort of pantheon of the Venetian Republic because so many Doges were buried there.

The Dominican Monks who lived in the two large cloisters, which are today part of the city hospital, exercised a great influence over the religious and social life of the city from the founding of the church in the thirteenth century up until the fall of the Republic.

Another important centre was the Church of the Pietá because of the charitable works for orphan children, but above all because of the work of the eighteenth-century composer and violinist Antonio Vivaldi. Carpaccio's painting cycle at the Scuola di San Giorgio degli Schiavoni and the Church and Convent of San Zaccaria are also of interest.

Corte del Milion.

Typical Canal.

Imaginary portrait of
Marco Polo.

Court with the open staircase
of the Morosini houses.

Large Cloister,
Convent of San Zaccaria.

Church of the Pietà.

Portrait of Antonio Vivaldi.

VENICE LAGOON

ISLANDS AND LITTORALS

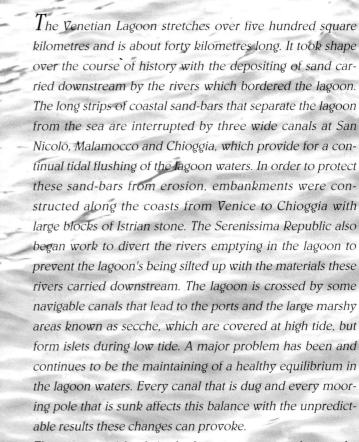

Lagoons.

The Venetian Lagoon stretches over five hundred square kilometres and is about forty kilometres long. It took shape over the course of history with the depositing of sand carried downstream by the rivers which bordered the lagoon. The long strips of coastal sand-bars that separate the lagoon from the sea are interrupted by three wide canals at San Nicolò, Malamocco and Chioggia, which provide for a continual tidal flushing of the lagoon waters. In order to protect these sand-bars from erosion, embankments were constructed along the coasts from Venice to Chioggia with large blocks of Istrian stone. The Serenissima Republic also began work to divert the rivers emptying in the lagoon to prevent the lagoon's being silted up with the materials these rivers carried downstream. The lagoon is crossed by some navigable canals that lead to the ports and the large marshy areas known as secche, which are covered at high tide, but form islets during low tide. A major problem has been and continues to be the maintaining of a healthy equilibrium in the lagoon waters. Every canal that is dug and every mooring pole that is sunk affects this balance with the unpredictable results these changes can provoke.

The are many islands in the lagoon, some are close to the city while others are farther away, some are important in terms of location and history while others which may have once been important have been swallowed up by the waters. Near the centre of Venice one finds the Giudecca, San Giorgio Maggiore, San Servilio and San Lazzaro degli Armeni. North of the city lie San Michele (now the cemetery), Murano, Mazzorbo, Burano, Torcello and San Francesco del Deserto. The Giudecca is divided from Venice by

Abandoned island.

Fishing in the Lagoon.

The lagoon, the island of S.Lazzaro degli Armeni, a stretch of the Lido,
the Adriatic, and in the background, the beach in the direction of Jesolo.

the Canal of the Giudecca and is really a group of eight islands. It has many rii (small canals) and calle (narrow streets) and was known for its delightful gardens and orchards. Andrea Palladio's masterpiece, the church of the Redentore lends its profile to the Giudecca. The Lido has always been closely linked with Venice; during the Fourth Crusade, the War with Genoa, and the Sensa when the Doge would symbolically "wed" the sea at the Church of San Nicolò. Many famous people have spent time on the Lido including Goethe, Byron, Shelley, De Musset and Théophile Gauthier. In the Protestant Cemetery lie the remains of Joseph Smith, the English collector who acquired most of the works by Canaletto that grace the walls of the museums of London. San Lazzaro degli Armeni with its church and library is of great cultural interest. There are also the islands of San Servilio, La Grazia, San Clemente and Sacca Sessola. The islands to the north of the lagoon are the best known. Torcello is believed to be one of the first settlements of refugees from the mainland. Burano is famous for lacemaking and Murano for glassworking. San Francesco del Deserto, accessible from Burano, has its own charming peace and solitude, and a small cloister that, legend has it, was visited by Saint Francis who landed there seeking shelter from a storm.

The islands and landscape of the Lagoon attract an ever-increasing number of visitors to this particular environment, with its variations of light and air heavily scented by the sea. In fact, Venice was born on these islands where Venetians learned the moves they needed to conquer the world.

167

FORMS
IN
GLASS

Murano is synonymous with glass, and a tour of a glass factory is par for the course. Murano glass is a handcrafted product from which are made various objects including coloured chandeliers, glasses, windows, mosaic tessere and groups of sculpted animals, like horses, dogs and so on. It is erroneous to say that Murano glass is all blown, even if this is the most common technique, employed for the transparency and near perfection it allows. Any irregularities in the glass are due to the speed with which the glass blower must work. He has very little

Glass making.

time to shape his molten lump of glass before it cools and hardens. The equipment necessary for the master glass maker and his assistants includes the furnaces, large melting pots, hollow tubes, steel pincers and other tools. The glass blowing is carried out in front of the furnace opening where the glass maker inserts the hollow tubes with molten glass on the end. This space just before the furnace, known as the piazza, is where he gives form to the glass by blowing into and simultaneously turning the pipe. He perfects the work with his pincers, constantly turning and blowing into the tube. When the glass hardens, the glass maker will reheat it and repeat the process until the work is finished. This often results in a noteworthy work of art. In addition to the glass factories, there are also several churches of interest in Murano. A visit to the Church of San Pietro Martire is also worthwhile: "*The Assumption of the Virgin with Saints and the Doge Agostino Barbarigo*" by Giovanni Bellini and "*St Agatha in Prison Visited by St Peter and an Angel*" by Paolo Veronese (left aisle).

The Glass Museum. The recently reorganized museum is an interesting place to visit to comprehend the evolution of glass blowing and the various forms developed over the course of history.

The Basilica of Santi Maria e Donato. This church was built in the twelfth century. Among its most important parts are the external apse-end, the twelfth-century mosaic floor and the stunning apse mosaic of the Virgin on a gold ground.

Visitors to Burano, like those to San Francesco del Deserto which can be reached from Burano, are generally more interested in the landscape and natural environment of this part of the lagoon than they are in works of art per se. A walk down the streets of Burano allows one to observe the perfect cohabitation of the population with the waters. The houses are modest one or two-storey buildings each of a different colour, and their doors are a oneness with street and canal. The Museum of Lacemaking. Lacemaking is a long process requiring great skill. Burano lace is hand-made and today produced in very limited quantities. In the Middle Ages and during the Renaissance, nuns in the city's countless convents made lace, praying as they worked. That lace was used primarily in churches as altar coverings and for priests' vestments.

BURANO AND LACE

Torcello can easily be spotted from both Burano and the mainland, recognizable from afar with its ancient belltower, which you almost feel you can reach out and touch. Today, Torcello is little more than a large square crowded with tourists, which however preserves two impressive though simple churches, quite small in size but with all the architectural elements of an ancient tradition. Refugees from Altino first settled in Torcello at the time of the Lombard invasions. The Cathedral was founded in 639, according to an inscription found there, and is considered by many to be the oldest building in the lagoon. It is a Byzantine building on a Romanesque-basilica plan. The ruins of a round seventh-century baptistery can be seen in front of the Cathedral. The Church of Santa Fosca stands next to it. The island has seen many changes, including a period when the inhabitants, newly threatened by invasion, decided to destroy their houses and move en masse to the Rialto, taking with them all their possessions including the very bricks of their houses. The type of brick used at the time, known as Torcellane, was made with straw and mud, and can still be found today in the nearby canals.

Views of Burano.

Torcello.
Cathedral
of Santa Maria Assunta.

Cathedral
of Santa Maria Assunta.
Interior.

LIDO

THE VENICE BEACH

The Lido is a long slim strip of land formed by the sedimentation of river detritus on the shallow sea floor. Within this natural dyke are the lagoon waters, which are in constant communication with the sea - entering by the three channels of S.Nicolò del Lido, Malamocco and Chioggia. There is an irregular ebb and flow of tides within the lagoon area and, since the city was founded, its lower levels have always been prone to flooding in certain periods of the year. The problem of high tides has grown in recent years because the flooding phenomenon is on the increase, and, no longer confined to the customary periods, causes major damage to the city and its inhabitants. Projects aimed to check the irregularity of tides and counter flooding are being implemented.

S.Lazzaro degli Armeni,
Lido and the port of S.Nicolò;
Punta Sabbioni and the beach in the
direction of Jesolo (background).

The island of S.Lazzaro degli Armeni.

San Pietro in Volta.

Lagoon Views.

MALAMOCCO, THE ALBERONI
SAN PIETRO IN VOLTA

BOAT EXCURSIONS

Malamocco is a fishing village, built after the sea had engulfed the ancient settlement of Matemaucus (1106-07), one of the two political centres of the first lagoon settlers.

Alberoni is a locality offering bathing establishments and a well-kept golf-course.

S.Pietro in Volta. The toponym Volta (voltare in Italian means "to turn") is linked to the locality where Pepin, son of Charlemagne, turned back after trying in vain to conquer Venice. It is the area of the littoral offering the best view of the Murazzi, the system of de-

fence against the sea erected by the Venetian Republic a few years before its demise in the eighteenth century. The Murazzi, formed of huge blocks of Istrian stone, are today buttressed with heaped concrete boulders to neutralize the impact and corrosion of breakers.

CHIOGGIA

THE FISHERMEN'S ISLAND

An excursion to Chioggia, whether by bus or by water-bus, provides the opportunity to take in the littoral, the Murazzi, should one stop off at S.Pietro in Volta, and the life of the fisherfolk. Chioggia today is a fishing port but tradition certainly dates back to Roman times. It was then called Fossa Clodia Major and Clodia Minor or Sottomarina. The Chioggian War (1378-80) was a turning point in the history of the Republic. Besieged by the Genoese fleet, and on the point of yielding, Venice made a last effort and was rewarded with victory. Among the ancient buildings in Chioggia, mention must be made of the church of S.Domenico, with Vit-tore Carpaccio's painting of St Paul (1520), the church of S.Giacomo and the Cathedral with its belltower. The Cathedral, with nave, two aisles and transept, is built on a Latin cross plan. Sottomarina is a modern seaside resort in constant evolution.

Views of Canal Vena.